우크라이나와 세계를
바라보며 Opinions *on*
　　　　　Ukraine *and* the World

우크라이나와 세계를 바라보며

2022년 4월 18일 초판 1쇄 발행
2022년 5월 23일 초판 2쇄 발행

지은이 조다윗

도서출판 비전출판사
주소 서울특별시 서대문구 홍은동 395-5 (03659)
전화 02-6414-7864
이메일 visionpd2@hanamail.net
홈페이지 www.wmuv.net
등록번호 제 312-2013-000011호

ISBN 979-11-87120-09-4 (03230)

© 조다윗 2022

Opinions *on* Ukraine *and* the World
by David Cho

Copyright © 2022, by David Cho

이 책의 저작권은 저자와 도서출판 비전출판사가 소유합니다.
신저작권법에 의하여 한국 내에서 보호를 받는 저작물이므로
무단전재와 복제를 금합니다.

Opinions *on* Ukraine *and* the World
Copyright 2022. Missionary David Cho and Vision Publishing House
all rights reserved.

우크라이나와 세계를 바라보며

Opinions *on* Ukraine *and* the World

조다윗 선교사 지음

비전선교단

차례

	머리말	9
	감사의 말	13
1	**서론** – 전염병 이후, 그리고 전쟁	15
2	**푸티니즘과 시진핑, 시황제 그리고 네로**	18
	1) 푸티니즘 체제 아래 우크라이나 전쟁 전개 가능성	22
	2) 시진핑, 시황제 등극을 위해 과연 대만을 제물로 삼으려 하는가 – 푸틴에 이은 시진핑의 전쟁 개전 가능성 요소 분석	30
3	**지정학적 전통에 입각한 군사대국 대^對 빅테크^{Big Tech}**	38
4	**전쟁의 피, 무고한 핏값, 협상과 휴전 그리고 평화의 가능성**	46
5	**결론** 우리의 책무 – 위기와 재앙 사이에서, 전망부재의 기독교인가? 비전의 기독교인가?	54
6	**함께 할 기도방향**	61
	참고도서 및 참조정보	64

Contents

	Preface	69
	Thanks to	73
1	Introduction - Post Pandemic, and the war	75
2	Putinism, Xi Jinping, Shi Huangdi(Ancient Chinese Emperor) and Nero	79
	1) Possibility of war progression in Ukraine under Putinism	84
	2) Is Xi Jinping trying to make Taiwan as his scapegoat to become Emperor Shi Huangdi? – Analysis of Xi Jinping's possibility of waging war following Putin	93
3	Big Tech vs. Russia, a military power based on geopolitical tradition	104
4	The blood of war, the price of innocent blood, the possibility of negotiations, truce, and peace	114
5	Conclusion Our responsibilities - Between crisis and disaster, Is Christianity without prospects? Is Christianity with a vision?	124
6	The direction of prayer to be with you	132
	Reference books and information	134

일러두기

이 글은 2022년 3월 경에 집필되었습니다.

『선교타임즈』 칼럼기고를 위해 칼럼형태의 글로 서두가 집필되기 시작하였음을 밝힙니다.

머리말

졸저가 될 것을 알면서도 우크라이나를 향한 글을 시급한 상황에서 급히 써내려간 연유가 몇 가지 있다.

이미 수년전 우크라이나와 러시아 간 분쟁의 조짐이 되었던 크림반도에는 우리가 20년째 품고 기도하고 있는 작은 민족이 있었다. 오래 이슬람을 믿어왔고 스탈린의 강제이주로 인구 3분의 2 가량이 죽어가며 중앙아시아로 끌려간 그 민족이, 국제학, 지역학 학자들에게도 존재가 잊혀져 사멸된 줄만 알았던 2000년 어간에, 크림반도로 귀환하여 민족의 실체가 있음이 그들에 불굴의 생존력으로 입증하였다.

그들이 귀환하였을 때 민족종교가 이슬람이었음에도 우크라이나 기독교국가로 돌아와 복음을 제한 없이 들을 수 있는 환경에 놓이게 되었음에도 그들을 향한 연구도, 국제사회에 그들의 정체성을 알리는 오피니언도 거의 존재하지 않아 20대에 선교비전을 품었던 청년시절부터 그들을 향한 기도모임의 마음이 연속된 게 오늘까지 이르러 개척한 비전선교단의 핵심 정신이 되었다. 기도가 유의미하여 그들을 향해 지속적으로 정탐·개척팀도 보내어보고 단기적으로도 복음을 받아들이는 현지인을 확인했으며, 그들이 고려인과 가깝게 지낸데다가 오순절 계통에 부흥이 있는 우크라이나 현지교회와 연결되면 2000년 동안 한 번도 복음을 듣지 못한 그들이 장기선교사 등에 접촉으로 복음화 될 수 있는 가능성을 지난 20년간 이 민족을 위해 기도하며 목도할 수 있었다.

그래서 이 책자는 우크라이나 침공에 대한 세계적 시의성 앞에 객관적 전망을 담으려 노력하면서도, 사실 개인적으로는 자책과 회개의 의도가 저변에 깔려있다. 두 세 사람이 모여 기도하고 복음으로 행전하면 2000여 년 동안 잃어버린 민족이 주께로 돌아와 구원과 평화를 얻으리라고 선포해왔는데, 시대적으로 깨어있지 못해 크림반도와 우크라이나 국가 전체를 분쟁과 살육의 전쟁으로 넘겨준 것은 아닌가 하는 슬픔과 반성이 담겨있다.

해서 러시아, 중국, 미국 등을 둘러싼 강대국 간의 구조적 충돌로 세계가 더욱 어둠에 휩쓸리기 전에 하나님나라로 돌이켜 그분의 복음과 평화의 진전이 믿음의 사람들을 통해 있게 하고자 선교사의 미력이나마 보태 글을 꾹꾹 눌러 내려 적었다. 잉크가 있다면 피같이 뿌려 쓰는 처절한 심령으로, 그러나 글의 외피는 냉정히 객관화하여 쓰려 애썼다.

몸 글에 밝힌 대로 이 글이 전염병과 전란의 연속으로 휩쓸려가는 세계에 대한 평화에 그리스도의 대사, 그리스도인의 공동행동과 섬김, 기도와 복음의 행전을 촉발시키는 작은 인화점이 되길 바란다.

따라서 이 책자는 물리적으로나 영적으로 그러한 공동연대·운동·섬김을 작은 파고처럼 연속 촉발시키는 방향으로 새벽이슬과도 같은 청년들과 함께 유포할 예정이다. 작은 파도여도 모여 계속 물결치면 대양도 움직이는 법이다.

『선교타임즈』의 칼럼 기고 요청으로 이 글이 시작되기도 했다. 시의적으로 대응이 급한 사안을 담은 글이라 역시 소셜 미디어로도 초고를 분절하여 내보내고 있었으나 우리 섬기는 스텝의 칼럼기고 분량체크 미스로 작은 칼럼이 보다 긴 글, 더 많은 용량의 책자가 되었다. 실수도 협력하여 선을 이루게 하시는 주님께서 우리가 시대와 세계를 향해 놓친 책무가 있다면 이 연속된 위기를 감지케 하는 성령님의 각성을 통해 다시 우리의 마음을 깨우시고 그리스도와 함께 행전케 하실 것이다.

2022년 3월 31일 조다윗 선교사

감사의 말

책이 나오기까지 많은 영감에 자양분이 되어 준 믿음의 선진들과 더불어, 교정과 편집 작업을 도와준 유경은 간사, 박혜지 간사, 고상한 북디자인을 해 준 권혁기 간사, 영문 번역을 맡아준 박시원 간사, 반하은 간사, 손은혜 간사, 비전 선교 공동체와 함께하는 350여명의 선교 사역자들 모두 감사하다.

말씀과 함께 살기 위해 공동체의 삶을 마다않고 더불어 함께 하는 아내와 은빛, 시후, 안녕이를 비롯한 가족들은 내 보석들이다. 우리가 아니더라도 누군가를 통해 주님이 어두운 시대를 밝힐 말씀의 횃불을 드실 것이나 말씀이 우리와 함께 하심에, 그래서 감사하다.

1 서론
– 전염병 이후, 그리고 전쟁

영국 출신 석학 니얼 퍼거슨(Niall Ferguson) 하버드대 교수가 세계 팬데믹 초중기, 사태 과정에 대해 기술한 『둠, 재앙의 정치학』 등에서 전염병 이후 전 지구적 재앙과 위기는 전쟁이 될 거라 예상했다. 2021년 이 예견은 비단 니얼 퍼거슨 만의 견해가 아니라 동시다발적이게도 많은 학자들의 공통된 시대적 전망이나 논점으로 부각되었다.

그는 신중하지만 확고하게 미국, 중국, 러시아, 등의 강대국 간 전염병 사태 이후 일방적 패권에 균열이 생기거나 그 경쟁 패권을 상대적으로 오판하면서 중국 대만 간 긴장 등을 중심으로 국가 간 전면전을 너머 문명 사이 세계 전쟁을 예상했다.[1] 질병 다음 전쟁이라는, 지구적 재앙의 예고는, 일면 러시아-우크라이나 전쟁에 관해 국가 간 전면전을 너머 여러 국가 사이에 세계대전 즉 문명 간 파괴적 전쟁이 될 수 있다는

---

[1] 11장과 결론에서 미국과 중국 간의 문제를 다루며 '새로운 냉전', '지정학적 재난' 등을 언급한다.
니얼 퍼거슨, 『둠 재앙의 정치학 (전 지구적 재앙은 인류에게 무엇을 남기는가)』, 홍기빈 옮김, 21세기북스(2021).

국제사회 간에 노심초사를 엿보건대,[2] 퍼거슨 교수의 시대적 전망이 절반 이상 이미 맞아 들어가는 것이 아닌가하는 불안감이 엄습해온다.

니얼 퍼거슨이 예고했던 앞으로 세계 간 본류의 갈등은 미국·러시아 간극을 일부 인정(역시 중국을 중심 갈등으로 포괄해)하면서도 미국·중국 간에 긴장이다.[3]

그의 예견에 질료가 되듯 중국 주석 시진핑이 임기 3기 집권을 다시 노리면서 임기 내에 대만문제를 반드시 해결하겠다 공언했다. 러시아-우크라이나 전쟁을 바라보며 대만 차이잉원 총통이 러시아 침공처럼 역시 중국도 대만을 위협하고 분열시키는 중이라 발언하기도하고 전군에 전투준비태세를 주문하기도 했으며 대만 시민 사회에는 "우크라이나 다음은 대만이다"라는 우려 섞인 구호가 퍼져나갔다.

앞으로 러시아-우크라이나 전쟁이 장기화되거나 이웃 몰도바, 조지아, 시리아, 체첸, 벨라루스, 폴란드, 리투아니아 등이 직간접 전쟁에 휩쓸린다면 서구 기독유업이 오래 머문 유럽 혹은 미주까지도 전쟁에 가담할 수 있다는 불안감이 없지

---

[2] 한스 페터 마르틴, 『게임 오버』, 이지윤 옮김, 한빛비즈(2020), p.433-436.
[3] Historian Niall Ferguson Predicts the Future of China. https://youtu.be/IIApVciCScw 2022.2.27

않다.[4] 만약 그렇게까지 되어간다면 우리 기독인들과 사역자들은 어찌해야 하겠는가?

혹 니얼 퍼거슨이 주목했던 중·미 간 대만을 둘러싼 갈등이 표면화되고 국제적 긴장이나 전쟁으로 번져간다면 대한민국, 북한, 일본, 러시아 등이 함께 인계철선으로 전쟁에 직간접적으로 휩쓸릴 가능성이 농후한데, 우리 그리스도인과 세계를 바라보는 선교사들은 앞에서는 전염병, 뒤에선 그림자 진 전쟁에 긴장을 바라보며 과연 무엇을 준비해야 할까?

△ 사진 1 **우크라이나 국기**

---

4 2014년 크림반도 합병 명목으로 푸틴은 러시아 '동족 보호'를 내세웠다. NATO 회원국들 중에 러시아인이 많이 거주하는 지역을 보유한 국가들이 여럿이다.
스티븐 리 마이어스, 『뉴 차르 (블라디미르 푸틴 평전)』, 이기동 옮김, 프리뷰(2016), p.662.

2 푸티니즘과 시진핑, 시황제 그리고 네로

현대 국가가 고대보다 복잡한 시스템이며 국가 경영 디시 즌 메이킹(decision making), 의사결정에 있어서도 다양한 요소를 고려하게 된다. 나라 간 총력을 기울이는 전쟁에 대한 결정도 마찬가지일 수 있다.

그럼에도 불구하고 러시아와 중국이 앞으로 확전하거나 전쟁을 계속 고수하거나 선택할 것이냐에 대한 전망은 다소 결정적 요소를 좁혀 생각할 수 있다.

왜냐하면 두 국가 모두 현대 시스템에서 몇몇 권력에게 의사결정이 집중되는 과두나 독재체제 양상을 띠고 있기 때문이다. 두 국가 모두 공산주의 일당 독재체제를 이어받아 집단 지도체제를 너머 소수나 독단적 인물에게 권력이 과독점되는 하이어라키, 파라미드 꼭짓점 구조의 정점을 달리고 있는 때이기도 하다.[5]

---

[5] 마르가레타 몸젠, 『푸틴 신디케이트 (비밀경찰 수중에 놓인 러시아)』, 이윤주 옮김, 한울(2019), p.6-7.

러시아와 중국이 현대국가지만, 공화정 또는 집단지도체제를 표방하였으나 마치 독재적 황제 네로나 도미티아누스가 출현했던 로마처럼, 러시아는 정보국 출신의 푸틴이 푸틴 자신을 정점으로 한 소수엘리트 관료, 군인, 독점 기업가 간 소수 네트워크를 바탕으로 '푸티니즘'이라고까지 불리는 장기 독재 체제를 구축했다.[6]

또한 중국, 시진핑 역시 변방으로 쫓겨난 고위급 관료의 자제였으나 특유의 신중한 처신으로 과두체제였던 중국 공산당 정점인 주석에 오르고 적폐청산을 명분으로 다른 결정적 과두 권력들을 제압하거나 견제해 일인독재체제의 바탕을 구축, 연임 이후의 집권기까지 권력을 연장하는 중국 전인대(전국인민대표대회) 헌법개정안을 통과시켰다.

사실상 종신직이 가능해 보이는 3기 집권의 문을 연 시진핑을 이제 국가 주석이 아닌 "시황제"라고 별칭하는 일이 논평가들 사이에 드물지 않다.

---

[6] 국가자본주의적 독재정치로 정의한다.
월터 라쿼, 『푸티니즘 (푸틴 열풍과 폭주하는 러시아)』, 김성균 옮김, 바다출판사 (2017), p.245.

△ 사진 2 Pray for Ukraine

이들이 독점적 권력을 구축한 채로 전쟁을 개전하거나 지속, 확대할 요소가 없지 않다는 것이 다수 학자들의 전망중론과 논점이 되고 있다.

그럼에도 불구하고 우리 기독인들은 네로황제를 성서적으로 하나님께서 어떤 관점으로 바라보셨는지 성경적 관점을 유비적으로 기준 삼는 것이 좋겠다. 로마서 집필 당시 위정자에게 순복하라고 말했던 바울의 권면(롬13:1)이 쓰인 AD 58년경은 아이러니하게도 네로의 집권기다. 또한 디모데전서에 임금들과 높은 지위에 있는 자들을 위해 기도하라고 했던 AD

65년경은 네로의 폭주가 정점을 향해 달려가고 있던 시기다.

하나님의 뜻을 거슬러 행할 네로 황제의 권력을 인정하고 악으로 세계와 기독교를 잔해할 네로를 위해 기도하라는 권면인 셈이다.

모든 권력 위에 권세를 주시고 모든 권세를 하나님나라의 권세로 수렴시킬 주권자이신 주님에 대한 믿음이 없다면 당시 그리스도인에게 불가능한 자세와 기도다.

네로가 예민한 신경증으로 대중영합을 추구해 사람들에 대한 거절을 두려워하고 스스로 어머니를 숙청하며 권세 아래 있는 자들을 함부로 대해 시민을 해할 방화를 조장, 누명을 기독교인에게 씌운 행태가 일어나가기까지 그의 악한 결정을 기독교인들이 주님께 기도하여 악을 보정하기를 구하게 하셨던 것이다. 당대의 기독인에게 네로를 위해 기도하라는 이런 권면은 꽤 불가해한 말씀일 수 있겠다. 주님은 네로의 악에 선택이나 폭주 직전에 보정할 기회를 주시나 AD 100년 앞 둔 계시록의 기록에서는 악을 선택한 네로를 666으로 반드시 평가하신다. 역사는 악을 택한 네로를 반드시 기억하고 대대로 평가했다. 이것이 하나님의 심판이요 곧 공의다.

이 글을 통해 현대의 푸티니즘과 시황제에 대해 분석할 터이나, 앞으로 전쟁이 확전되고 계속될지 또 다른 국가 간 전면전이나 문명 간 세계대전이 치러질는지 더 알 수 없는 상황이다. 악한 선택에 근접한 체제나 국제 정세 등을 위해서도 기도해야 할 일이지만, 그 방아쇠 트리거가 될 수 있는 푸틴과 시진핑이 전쟁이나 확전을 선택할 수도 있는 유혹 요소를 분석할 것이다. 더불어 그들이 악의 트리거를 선택하기 전에 주님의 주권과 맞닿아 있는 성도들이 반드시 한마음으로 기도하는 일이 매우 절실하다. 그들은 그들 스스로의 선택을 하겠으나 그들 결정으로, 세계시민과 민족들이 수많은 고통에 휩싸이게 됨을 깊이 염두에 두고 아직 다 선택되지 않아 전개되지 않은 악의 양을 생각할 때, 오히려 우리의 기도의 부담은 지금 굉장히 커야만 한다. 지금이 세계를 향한 기도에 크리티컬 타임이다.

1) 푸티니즘 체제 아래 우크라이나 전쟁 전개 가능성

푸틴이 장기적으로 구축한 독재체제가 소련 붕괴 이후

KGB 출신이었던 푸틴의 출신 성분상 공산주의의 은밀한 권위주의적 구조의 통치 문화를 이어간 것은 사실이다. 그러나 푸티니즘은 구소련처럼 단일 구성요소의 독재체제라기보다는, 비밀정보국 출신 엘리트 인사들, 관료들, 정부의 비호와 후광을 받는 독과점기업가들 간 포스트 전체주의체제 상 푸틴이 꼭짓점에 있는 것이다. 아울러 그의 장기 집권 바탕은 대중영합에 부응한 측면이 있다.[7]

소련의 붕괴 이후 강대국의 위상을 회복하길 원했던 러시아 대중의 염원에 소구해, 푸틴이 소련 이후 무너졌던 러시아의 경제력을 에너지 자원의 수출·개발 등을 통해 부흥시킨 바탕에서 그의 독재장기집권 정당성이 마련되었다.[8] 따라서 우크라이나 침공에도 그의 국민적 지지율이 여전히 65% 이상이라는 언론보도는 결코 프로파간다만은 아닐 것이다.

---

[7] 마르가레타 몸젠, 앞의 책(2019), p. 85, 104.
[8] 푸틴의 집권 시기는 페트로스테이트(petroleum석유 + state국가의 합성어로 산유국 혹은 석유천연가스로 상당한 자본을 축적하고 독점하는 권력 형태의 국가들을 의미한다)에 적용된다.
월터 라쿼, 앞의 책(2017), p.400-403.

△ 사진 3 블라디미르 푸틴(Влади́мир Пу́тин) 러시아 대통령

그러할 진데 푸틴이 이번 무리한 전쟁을 통해 러시아 국력을 완전히 소모하고 국제제재 등의 난관을 만나 푸티니즘 체제가 전복될 수 있다는 서방의 관측이나 염원은 그들 자체적인 시각일 가능성이 있다. 전염병 사태 가운데 '자유가 우선이냐 사회 보건 질서가 우선이냐'의 방역정책에 따라 분열했던 서구사회가 이번 대러시아 제재로 단일대오로 규합된 측면이 있긴 하다. 하지만 이번 국제제재에는 서구 동맹을 제외한 중국, 인도, 중동, 남미 다수 국가 등이 참여하지 않아 세계 절반 이상이 제재국면에 동참하지 않았음도 엄연한 현실이다.

또한 설령 푸틴이 제거된다 해도 러시아 대중에 영합한 푸틴의 리더십을 대리할 또 다른 강력한 지도력 상을 군중이 바라고, 푸틴 주변에 비슷한 통치문화를 습득한 엘리트와 대안 인물이 부상할 가능성이 농후하다.

물론 푸틴은 우크라이나 침공 전쟁 개전 초기 우크라이나 국민의 극렬한 저항을 만나 친러의 괴뢰정부를 세우는 본인들 목적을 아직까지 이루지 못하고 소모전을 치루고 있다. 그러나 이러한 소모 때문에 세계 2위 군사대국이자 에너지 강국이 전쟁을 치를 전력과 병참이 없어 초전에 나가떨어지리라는 예상도 성급한 사태 예단일 수 있다.

사실 우크라이나가 러시아를 제외하면 유럽에서 영토가 가장 큰 나라이고, 그들의 항전의지로 전쟁을 소모전으로 이끌어간 측면이 있지만 우크라이나 정부의 초전 붕괴를 유도하지 못한 러시아는 기존에 늘 본인들이 써왔던 전술대로 전쟁을 계속 치러내고 있다.

조지아, 시리아, 체첸, 몰도바, 리투아니아, 벨라루스 등지에서 보여주었던 러시아의 영향력 확보는 현 우크라이나 전쟁에 소모전과 궤가 유사하거나 거의 같다.[9] 영토 주변과 일부에 친러부대나 러시아 군대를 주둔시키고 저항요소가 보이면 그 주둔을 매개로 내전유도나 전쟁개전도 불사해 분할하여 결국 러시아에 승인받은 위성정부를 세우거나 친러 자치공화국을 세워왔다.

서방이 못 본 척하거나 개입하지 않았던, 비교적 국가단위보다 규모가 작은 자치공국이나 약소국에 있어 이미 실행해왔던 폭력에 영향력을 확대해, 보다 크고 비교적 더 서구와 맞닿아있는 우크라이나에서 이미 그대로 분할, 전복, 위성 지배의 전략을 그대로 실행, 전개 중이다.[10]

더군다나 우크라이나 남부 크림반도와 동부 루한스크, 도네츠크 축선을 잇는 마리우폴 같은 도시 전체를 포위, 무차별 포격으로 시민까지 식수·식량 고갈과 접근이 난망해지는 고립을 유도하고 항복을 받아내며, 시장 등을 친러 인사로

---

9 한양대 아태지역연구센터, 『유라시아 지역의 국가, 민족 정체성』, 한울아카데미 (2010) p.185, 224-225.

10 조지 프리드먼, 『다가오는 유럽의 위기와 지정학 (브렉시트, 유럽연합의 와해 그리고 독일 문제의 재부상)』, 홍지수 옮김, 김앤김북스(2020), p.210.

교체해내는 전략은 이미 우크라이나 남부, 동부를 이어 친러 영토로 새롭게 재편해내는 분할에 현 소모전 하에서도 폭력을 - 초전 예기치 못한 극렬한 저항으로 지연하였을 뿐 - 착실히 실행중이다. 그래서 러시아의 침공, 물리적 폭력의 영향력이 쉽게 좌절되리라는 예측이나 선전도 쉬 예단해서는 안 될 일이다. 푸틴과 러시아의 우크라이나 침공이 노린 물리적 폭력의 목적과 의도는 이미 우크라이나를 할퀴고 쉽게 수그러들지 않아 절반의 소기 목적을 달성해 가고 있는 중이다.

△ 사진 4 **러시아의 우크라이나 침공 전황**

그러나 푸틴이 물리적 침공과 폭력에서 절반의 성공, 절반의 패착을 가져온다하더라도, 푸틴과 러시아는 정신적인 문명사에 있어서는 거의 완패할 가능성이 농후해져가고 있다.

다시 말해 과거 러시아의 영향력을 갈망하는 푸티니즘 체제는 물리적 폭력 전투에 있어서는 소기에 성취를 가질 수도 있겠으나 문명 정신사에 있어서는 큰 패배나 패착에 수렁으로 빠져들고 있다는 느낌을 지울 수 없다. 히브리대 교수 하라리(Yuval Noah Harari)[11]의 견해처럼 러시아가 2차 대전에 스탈린그라드를 만나기까지 연전연승했던 독일군의 패착을 그대로 따르고 있다고 볼 수 있다. 러시아 소련의 전성기가 열릴 수 있었던 바탕과 배경은, 공산주의체제가 모순 없이 잘 기능해서 유지되었다고 보기보다는, 그 역사적 착수지점이 절대강국 독일에게 수세에 몰리다가 범국가적, 국민적 단결에 따라 독일군을 스탈린그라드에 진입시키고도 집요한 항전, 시가전을 통해, 설령 독일이 도시 전체를 막대히 부수어도, 저항을 포기치 않아 결국 물러나게 했던 러시아의 승리

---

[11] Yuval Noah Harari, 「Why Vladimir Putin has already lost this war」, 『The Guardian Weekly』, 2022.03.28., https://www.theguardian.com/commentisfree/2022/feb/28/vladimir-putin-war-russia-ukraine

신화에 기반한다.[12]

    아이러니하게도 이번 침공으로 우크라이나가 러시아의 일방적 침공과 폭력에 동남부, 북부 등이 노출되었을지라도 그들의 끈질긴 저항이 도리어 대국 러시아를 맞선 국가 근간 정신성으로 자리 잡을 것이다.

    석학 에릭 홉스봄(Eric Hobsbawm)의 견해와 같이 신화와 공동구성원 공통의 이미지에 따라 결집이 이루어지는 근현대국가 특성상,[13] 러시아에 끈질기게 저항하고 있는 우크라이나 민족 정신성이 문명사적으로 우크라이나인들의 국가적 정신성을 더욱 강화할 수 있다. 설령 러시아가 물리적 폭력에 있어서는 완연한 힘을 쏟고 우크라이나를 몰아붙여도, 대게 그들의 폭력이 우크라이나 도시들을 할퀴고 점령해도, 폭압

---

[12] 러시아인들은 이 전투가 그들의 위대한 애국 전쟁의 가장 위대한 전투 중 하나라고 생각하고 있으며, 대부분의 역사학자들은 이 전투가 전체 분쟁의 가장 위대한 전투라고 생각한다.
림바흐, 레이몬드. "스탈린그라드 전투". 브리태니커 백과사전, 2021년 8월 15일, https://www.britannica.com/event/Battle-of-Stalingrad, 2022년 4월 6일에 액세스함.

[13] 에릭 홉스봄, 『1780년 이후의 민족과 민족주의 (창비신서 125)』, 강명세 옮김, 창작과비평사(1998), p.68.
베네딕트 앤더슨, 『상상의 공동체 (민족주의의 기원과 전파에 대한 성찰)』, 윤형숙 옮김, 나남(2003), p.25

을 비대칭적으로 당하여도, 장기적 문명 정신성으로는 푸티니즘과 러시아를 압도하고 승리할 가능성이 높아 보인다.

2) 시진핑, 시황제 등극을 위해 과연 대만을 제물로 삼으려 하는가 – 푸틴에 이은 시진핑의 전쟁 개전 가능성 요소 분석

소련 몰락 이후 푸틴은 원래 집권초기 유럽 정체성에서 흡사 동로마 중심으로 러시아를 상정하고 EU와 NATO(북대서양조약기구)에 우호적인 외교접근을 시행하였다. 심지어 옐친에 이어 NATO와 EU에 러시아를 진입시켜 서구와 함께하려는 외교 스탠스도 보였다.[14] 그러나 집권 중기를 지나며 푸틴이 서구 유럽 친화성에서 러시아의 정체성의 근간을 찾는 대신 유라시아 대륙 역사성에서 러시아의 정체성을 찾으려하여 서방과 역사 정체성의 각을 세우기 시작했다. 그 요인 중 하나로 서구의 프라이드 패착이 한몫을 하였다.

---

[14] 마르가레타 몸젠, 앞의 책(2019), p.153-154.

집권초기 푸틴의 친서구적 태도에 NATO나 EU의 핵심국들은 러시아를 몰락한 소련의 후신으로 격을 낮추어보는 것이 대체적 시각이었고 그 바탕 가운데 외교적으로 몰락한 소련으로서 러시아라는 미국과 서구의 일방적 관점으로 대우했다. 이러한 시각은 세계 제2위의 군사대국으로서 경제부흥까지 꿈꿔온 푸틴 입장에서는 용납하기 어려운 하대였다. 그 후 여전히 러시아정교회의 어용화(御用化)를 통해 동로마 제국의 후신임을 강조하면서도 집권 중기 이후 푸틴은 미주 유럽을 포괄하는 서방, 즉 서로마와의 친화보다는 유라시아 대륙 정체성으로서 러시아와 아시아를 잇는 정체성으로 서구와의 역사적 변별성을 설정하고 곧 대립각을 세우기 시작했다.[15]

여기에서 신중한 시진핑에게 중국몽(中國夢)과 G1의 세계 패권을 향한 과감한 긴장, 국제 갈등도 불사할 일말과 연속의 스탠스, 자세를 열어주게 되었다고 해도 과언이 아니다. 중국은 만만디(慢慢的) 정신에 따라 패권국가가 되기 전에는 발톱을 드러내지 않는다는 전략적 패권질서 접근이 강한 국가

---

15 서구는 처음부터 반러시아 정책을 추구하며 러시아를 서구에 기술적, 경제적으로 의존하는 반식민지로 변화시키고파했다.
월터 라퀴, 앞의 책(2017), p.375-376.

다.[16] 또한 그에 따라 미국과의 일대일 긴장관계도 되도록 패권이 완벽히 장악되기 전에 부각되는 것을 조심해왔다. 그럼에도 아시아의 갈등 긴장 대립항의 세계 요소를 이해하는 관점은 서구적 관점에 일대 일의 양자대립보다 가위바위보게임과 같은 삼자대립항으로 이해하는데에 더욱 능한 편이다.

서방이 비교적 친서구정책을 집권초기에 가졌던 푸틴과 러시아를 적극적으로 국제현실정치 요소로 존중, 포용치 못하고 대립항으로 놓치게 됨으로써, 시진핑과 중국은 러시아를 패권질서의 대립항을 미국 대(對) 중국으로만 보지 않고 미국 대 중국 러시아의 삼원대립항으로 접근하게 할 수 있는 계기를 연 셈이다.

일찍이 시리아내전으로 시아파의 알 아사드 독재정권, 정부군을 적극 도와 군사 원조했던 러시아와 수니파를 아우르는 자유시리아 반군에 섰던 미국은 오히려 시리아 내부에 독재정권을 강화하고 미국이 지원했던 자유시리아 수니파 반군에서 기회를 얻어 파생된 다에시, IS가 이슬람극단주의 체제로 중동에 자리 잡게 했다.[17]

---

16   한스 페터 마르틴, 앞의 책(2020), p.138-152
17   제라르 샬리앙, 소피 무세, 『쿠르드 연대기 (IS 시대의 쿠르드족 문제)』, 은정 펠스너 옮김, 한울(2018), p.152.

미국이 의도했건, 무지했던 간에 미국이 지원한 수니파 반군에서 파생·출현해 영향력을 확대한 IS는 현상적으로는 일대일로[18]를 꿈꿔 중동 내에 교역로를 열려고 했던 중국몽에 타격을 입히게 했다.[19] 쿠르드민족이 살고 있는 터키, 시리아, 이란 국경 근방으로 IS가 자리 잡으면서 중국이 야심차게 추진했던 일대일로 중동 교역로는 체제 혼란과 이슬람 극단주의 기승으로 병목 교착화되거나 아예 막히게 되었다.[20]

미국의 아프간 철군 역시 중국을 제일 주적으로 여겨 중국과의 대결에 집중하고자 한 결과의 부산물이다. 미국은 아프간 자치정부의 자립할 수 없을 정도에 만연한 부패를 잘 알고 있는 측면이 있었다. 그런 무능한 아프간 자치정부 상황 하에서 미군이 철수한다면 탈레반이 자치정부를 전복시키고, 체제 접거할 수 있을 것이란 점 또한 충분히 예상할 수 있었

---

[18] 일대일로(一帶一路) 프로젝트는 대규모 토목 사업으로, 2030년까지 동서남아시아와 중앙아시아를 넘어 유럽과 아프리카를 육로와 해로로 잇고 도로, 항만, 철도, 산업단지를 건설하여 주변 65개국을 아울러 경제권을 구축하는 것을 목표로 한다.

[19] KBS 다큐 인사이트 팬데믹 머니 제작팀, 『팬데믹 머니』, 리더스북(2021), p. 217.

[20] 제라르 샬리앙, 앞의 책(2018), p.168-169.

다.[21] 그럼에도 불구하고 수많은 미국산 군사장비를 아프가니스탄에 놓아둔 채 미국이 철군한 아리송한 이유에 대해, 중국 서부 신장위구르 등이 극단 이슬람주의 활동 무대가 된다면 탈레반과 함께 연결, 연대하여 중국을 견제할 요소가 된다는 전망으로, 일부러 탈레반 수중에 넘어갈 수 있는 미군사무기를 버려두고 어설픈 철수를 했다는 시각조차 있다.

또한 이라크전쟁을 통해 사담 후세인이 미국에게 견제 받다 못해 몰락한 요인이 후세인이 과감하게 석유를 달러가 아닌 화폐로 매매하면서 미국 패권에 도전한 것에 대한 미국의 응징이라는 관점도 있다. 시진핑은 이미 원유를 달러가 아닌 위안화로 거래하는 산유국과의 거래노선을 구체적으로 시행, 설정했다.[22]

시진핑이 대 국제사회를 향해 전망했던 중국몽도 일장춘몽으로 끝날 가능성이 높아지고 있다. 2030년대 이후 중국 패권이 미국보다 앞설 것이라는 일부 전망도 일대일로의 후퇴

---

21 이근욱, 『아프가니스탄 전쟁』, 한울아카데미(2021), p.405, 425.
22 KBS 다큐 인사이트 팬데믹 머니 제작팀, 앞의 책(2021), p. 224.

나 지지부진, 중국내 관치금융-그림자금융의 모순 누적, 경기호황 선전을 위한 막대한 유령도시건설의 실패 등으로 G1으로 올라갈 국력이나 세계 국제 어젠다 성취가 대체로 소실되거나 전망치가 밝지 못하게 되었다.

중국과 시진핑은 대외 국제적으로는 대 미국과 패권경쟁에 있어 갈등과 긴장 충돌 요소가 피할 수 없을 정도로 무르익어가고 있음을 인지하고 있고,[23] 주창해왔던 세계 어젠다 설정에 난망과 소진을 겪고 있다. 따라서 이같은 현실국제정치 상황 하에서 3기 집권정당성 마련과 국가적 결집을 위해 내부적 민족주의 요소 부각으로 중국정체성을 세울 가능성이 점점 높아져간다고 니얼 퍼거슨은 전망한다.[24]

즉 대만과의 오래된 갈등 관계 재설정, 즉 양안이 하나의 중국이라는 시각을 국제적으로 관철하려 나설 가능성을 시진핑이 염두에 두고 있다는 얘기다. 중국 혼자 미국을 대립하

---

[23] 공민석, 『미중 갈등의 구조(금융 위기 이후의 헤게모니 경쟁, 북 저널리즘)』, 스리체이어스(2019), p.89-96.

[24] Historian Niall Ferguson Predicts the Future of China. https://youtu.be/llApVciCScw 2022.2.27

기에는 신중한 시진핑의 성격상 혹은 중국의 만만디 정신 상 어려워도, 이미 미국 패권질서에 도전한 이상 갈등과 충돌은 불가피하다. 또 다른 군사대국 러시아가 우크라이나 전쟁 등을 통해 미국과 대립해주거나 국력을 소모해줄 때, 중국의 전쟁 개전 유혹 가능성은 더 높아질 수도 있겠다. 집권 2기를 이어 사실상 종신도 가능한 내년 2023년 3기를 인정받고 열어가야 할 시진핑의 시황제 변모를 염두에 둘 때, 2022년 시진핑이 대만문제를 해결하겠다고 공언한대로 전쟁 개전에 유혹을 뿌리칠 수 없을지도 모른다.[25] 또한 이미 우크라이나 전쟁 상 고급정보들이 유출되며 나타난 대로 푸틴은 베이징 동계 올림픽 이후 우크라이나 전쟁을 개전하기로 시진핑과 교감, 소통, 통보, 사전 조율을 거쳤으며 외교상호주의 원칙에 입각하여 시진핑도 2022년 올해 가을, 대만을 침공하겠노라 푸틴과의 회담에서 소통한 것으로 나타나고 있다.[26]

러시아의 침공으로 개전된 우크라이나 전쟁이 우크라이

---

[25] 조용성, 『중국의 미래 10년』, 넥서스 BIZ(2012), p.110.
[26] 2022년 2월 4일, 시진핑 중국 국가주석과 블라디미르 푸틴 러시아 대통령은 베이징에서 정상회담을 갖고 북대서양조약기구(NATO)의 확장 중단을 촉구하는 공동 성명을 발표했다. 이 회담에서 중국은 우크라이나의 나토 가입 반대를 지지했고, 러시아는 대만독립 반대하며 주요 국제 문제에 만장일치된 입장을 표명했다.

나의 결사항전으로 러시아를 소모전으로 이끌어 미국을 비롯 서구 사회는 대리전을 치를 뿐 소모전에 크게 직접 개입되지 않았다는 점, 그럼에도 러시아가 크림 반도와 루한스크, 도네츠크 지역을 잇는 교두보지역, 마리우폴 함락을 눈앞에 두어 영토적으로는 이미 우크라이나를 분할 점령할 가능성 높아졌다는 양면적 국면이 있다는 점에서, 신중한 시진핑이 대만을 결국 침공, 대미 갈등을 더욱 수면 위에 부상시켜 국제전쟁화할지 쉽게 예단할 수만은 없다. 또한 전쟁이 전혀 없을 것이라고 냉혹한 국제질서를 낙관적으로만 전망할 수도 없겠다. 다만 세계시민이 고통과 암울에 휩싸일 대만 침공과 세계대전만큼은 일어나지 않기를 바라고 간절히 기도할 뿐이다.

△ 사진 5 **시진핑(Xi Jinping) 중국 대통령 과 조 바이든(Joe Biden) 미국 대통령**

3 지정학적 전통에 입각한 군사대국 러시아 대^對 빅테크^{Big Tech}[27]

러시아가 이번 전쟁을 개전함에 있어 미국보다 핵탄두를 많이 보유한 세계 제2위의 군사대국이라 할 만한 면모를 보이기는커녕, 현대 전쟁의 기초 문법조차 망각한 채 막무가내식 서투른 전투를 치르는 것이 아닌가하는 시각이 있다. 현대전에 있어 전쟁을 유리하게 끌고 가기 위해서는 전쟁 지역에 통신과 방송 등을 장악하거나 마비시키는 것이 중요하다. 그럼에도 전쟁이 소모전을 너머 장기전 태세로 넘어갈 수 있어 보이는 현재 전개 상황에 이르기까지, 우크라이나에 전황 소식, 시민 사회, 정부 가버넌스와 국제사회 대응 등이 실시간으로 공유되고 있다. 전란 중에 레거시 언론·방송·통신이 당연히 장악 혹은 마비 된 것이 아니라, 도리어 개인 스마트폰의 카메라들이 어디에서나 1인 방송으로 우크라이나 곳곳에서 일어나는 전쟁 상황을 세계에 송출하였다. 이로써 전쟁이라는 국가 비상사태 중에도 공영 방송의 정보 취합 영역보다

---

27 디지털 플랫폼을 보유하고 운영하는 대형 기술(IT) 기업. 뒤에 참고도서 및 서지정보 참고.

훨씬 방대한 실시간 현장과 정보들이 세계 곳곳으로 퍼져나가고 있다.

러시아는 과연 전쟁을 일으키면서 상대국의 통신 방송 등을 장악하거나 파괴해야 전쟁을 유리하게 끌고 갈 수 있다는 현대전의 원리를 간과할 만큼, 아마추어처럼 전황을 패착으로 끌어가고 있는 것일까? 이러한 현대전의 문법을 러시아가 간과했다기보다는 세계 제2의 군사대국이자 지정학적 강대국인 나라조차 빅테크에, 어떠한 면에서는 지정학적 국가권력을 능가하는 능력에 당하고 있다고 봐도 무방하다. 러시아는 초전에 우크라이나 통신과 방송 시스템을 폭파하거나 단절 장악하려는 시도를 물론 했음이 분명하다.

그런데도 우크라이나의 다소 젊은 30대 부총리가 초전에 트위터로 매우 정중히 일론 머스크(테슬라 창업주)에게 공개적으로 저공 위성 통신시스템인 '스타링크'를 우크라이나 상공에 띄워 줄 것을 요청했다. 이에 일론 머스크 역시 트위터로 간단명료한 긍정의 응답을 남김으로써 우크라이나 국가 내에 기간 통신과 방송 설비 뿐만이 아닌, 우주상에 인공위성 시스템을 통해 우크라이나 영토 내에 인터넷과 통신, 스마

트폰에 기반한 개인 방송 등이 전란 중에도 여전히 가능케 되었다.[28]

전 지구적 코로나 전염병 사태에도 일론 머스크를 비롯한 소위 빅테크 그룹은 대규모 경기부양으로 화폐가 가치가 낮아지는 와중에도 도지코인, 비트코인, 이더리움, 알트코인 등으로 화폐가치를 우회하여 대안 가치로서 금에 준하는 코인시장을 운영했다. 그리하여 국가 권력을 우회하는 양상의 대안화폐로서 코인시장에 마음껏 활력을 불어넣고 거의 도박에 가까운 등락폭을 주도했다. 사실 일론 머스크가 도지코인, 일명 개를 심볼로 한 코인을 선택해서 팬덤과 그의 주도적 IT 기술에 대한 사회적 저명과 신뢰를 이용하여 소위 '개'코인에 거품 같은 활력을 불어넣다 빼기를 반복할 때는 그가 한심스러워 보이기도 했다.

그럼에도 이런 류의 빅테크 기업과 관련 엘리트들은 국가권력의 총체가 전염병에 대응해도 역부족인 상황하에서조차 도리어 초국가적 테크놀로지 플랫폼을 더욱 공교히 하여 전염병 사태로 어마어마한 반사 이익을 얻거나 쌓을 수 있었다.

---

[28] https://www.bbc.com/ukrainian/news-60583913

다시 말해 전 지구적 전염병 사태에 강대 선진 국가권력 조차 총력을 투여해도 사회적 소거, 대응 외에 거의 2년간 COVID-19 대 인류대응능력이 함양될 때까지 바이러스 사태에 대해 해결이 난망한 지점이 많았다.

그 와중에 전염병 사태로 비접촉 거리두기 사회가 보편화되면서 IT플랫폼에 기반한 빅테크들이 메타버스 등을 외치며 인류의 오소리티(authority)를 블랙홀처럼 빨아들이려 애썼으며 인류의 미래 사회 플랫폼·어젠다를 선점했다.

전염병 사태 이후 혹은 와중에 터진 이번 우크라이나 침공에서 막대한 군사대국 러시아에게 큰 타격을 입힌 제 일 공신 중 하나는 일론 머스크, 빅테크 기업 엘리트라 해도 과언이 아니다. 스타링크는 그가 오지까지 커버 가능한 인터넷보급을 위해 돌출적으로 창안·실행한 아이디어이다. 이 위성시스템은 지구 상공에 저고도로 도는 인공위성들을 촘촘히 띄워서 전 지구적으로 어느 곳에서도 빠른 인터넷이 가능케 하는 돌출적 아이디어도 아이디어지만 이런저런 부작용과 부수적 문제를 양산하는 계획이기도 했다.

지구대기 밖 우주 고위도에 위성을 띄우면 커버리지가 넓어 전 지구를 커버할 위성의 개수를 줄일 수 있으나, 원거리에서 통신을 주고받는 문제 때문에 속도가 현격히 저하된다. 일론 머스크는 돈키호테 스타일같이 저돌적이며 돌출적으로 지구 위 저고도에 수많은 위성을 띄워 빠른 인터넷 속도가 보장되는 시스템을 구현하려했다.

시간이 지나면 위성의 수명이 다해 수많이 양산 될 우주 쓰레기는 아이디어 구현 우선순위에서 고려 밖 부수적 요소일 뿐이었다. 또한 위성 간 충돌이 일어날 수 있는 뜻밖의 사고확률이 높아진다는 점, 자연과학 연구를 위한 천체 관측이 너무 많이 띄워놓은 위성 때문에 방해받는 상황도 괘념치 않았다. 우주는 어차피 지정학적 영토처럼 국가권력이 미치거나 점유하는 영역이 아니었다. 국가 권력 밖의 우주에 일론 머스크는 일종의 제한받지 않는 테크놀로지를 구축한 셈이다.

그런 일론 머스크가 창안한 스타링크라 불리는 지구 대기권 밖 지정학적 영공이나 영토 밖에 있는 인공위성에 기반한 통신시스템이 우크라이나 상공에 머물러 인터넷 통신이 계속되었다. 그럼으로써 우크라이나는 대러시아 침공에 맞서, 흡사 골리앗과 다윗의 싸움에 비견될 만한 전쟁에서, 자국에 유리한 소통으로 국가내부를 결집시켜 대 저항능력을 극대화하고 국제사회에 끊임없이 전황을 알리고 항전의지와 원조를 구할 수 있게 되었다. 스타링크는 그런 의미에서 우크라이나에게 골리앗을 쓰러트린 다윗의 물맷돌이라 해도 과언이 아니겠다.[29]

    우크라이나는 스타링크 등을 통해 실시간 인터넷·통신 등이 마비, 두절되지 않은 채로 전쟁에 임함으로써 실시간 침공상황을 세계에 틱톡, 유튜브, 페이스북, 인스타그램으로 생중계하다시피 할 수 있었다. 정부와 대통령을 비롯한 요직의 인물들도 스마트폰 하나면 국제 회담·회의 등에 실시간으로 침공의 부당성을 알리며 국제사회의 구원을 요청하며 원조를 끌어낼 수 있었으며, 미국으로부터 러시아의 실시간 침략 상황을 제공받았다. 또 시민들은 러시아가 점령한 헤르손 등 여러 지역에서 비폭력 저항 운동을 벌이면서, 러시아 군의 실시간 전범 상황 등을 채증할 수 있는 도구로 여전히 살아있는 인터넷 통신을 기반한 스마트폰 카메라를 각자 열어 틱톡, 유튜브, 페이스북 라이브, 인스타그램 등으로 도시를 점령한 러

---

29 글로벌협력본부, 「디지털로 바라본 우크라이나-러시아 사태」, 한국지능정보사회진흥원(2022), p.11.

시아 군대와 전차 등 중화기 앞에서 담대히 비폭력 시민 항쟁을 전개할 수 있게 되었다.

전염병과 전쟁 사태를 동시에 통과하며 빅테크 기업이 전통적 국가 권력을 우회하거나 비등 혹은 상회하는 시대를 예상, 전망해본다.[30] 비슷한 현상을 위협으로 느끼는 중국정부는 이러한 빅테크 기업이 일정부분 기술을 국가의 국익으로 향상시키기까지 제재나 규제 없이 두는 편이나, 국가 권력을 상회할 만큼 독보적으로 커지는 상황이 올 수 있다 싶으면 알리바바처럼 일종의 연착륙을 명목으로 견제하거나 국가 권력 앞에 귀속, 길들이기에 들어가고 심지어 준 해체에 이르게 한다. 세계 5분의 1 가량의 인구, 14억 명을 다스리는 중국 국가정부에게도 때론 국가 권력을 상회할 수 있어 보이는 빅테크 기업이 견제 대상으로 떠오른 셈이다. 세간 앞에서 러시아의 푸틴에게 일론 머스크가 소셜 미디어를 통해 결투를 신청하기도 했으며, 이미 한판 붙었다는 논평도 그냥 시쳇말로 치부하기엔, 이번 스타링크의 역할을 제압하지 못하고 통신을

---

30 일론 머스크의 스타링크 지원 이후 소셜 미디어 플랫폼 기업들은 우크라이나에 대한 가짜뉴스가 퍼지는 것을 막기 위해 러시아 관영 언론을 차단하거나 표식을 부착하는 등 러시아 제재에 나서고 있다.

주도적으로 장악하지 못한 채 전투가 흘러간 것이 러시아 군에게 큰 패착 요인이 된 점을 부인할 수 없겠다. 시대가 전염병과 전쟁 이후로 거대한 시프트 전환에 조짐이 일어나고 있음도 러시아의 우크라이나 침공과 그 패착을 통해 한 켠에서 확인, 예감해본다.

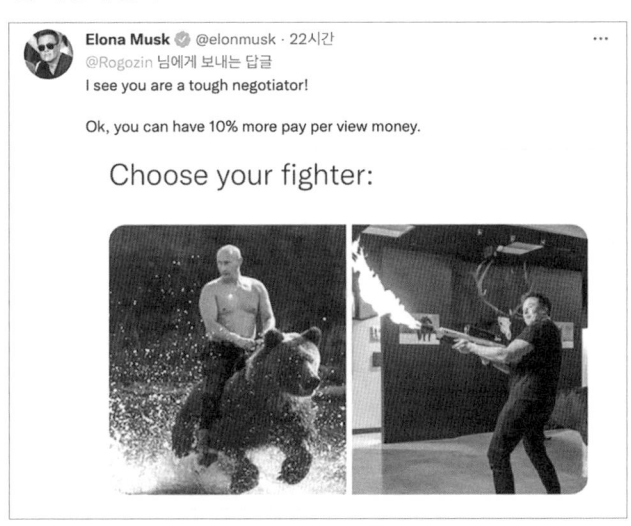

△ 사진 6 **일론 머스크(Elon Musk) 테슬라 CEO의 트윗**

4 전쟁의 피, 무고한 핏값, 협상과 휴전 그리고 평화의 가능성

우크라이나 땅에 뿌려진 무고한 핏값의 무게를 가만히 그러나 처절하게 달아보고 재어본다. 마리우폴 등지에서 죽어간 무고한 우크라이나 시민과 초전에 훈련인 줄만 알고 야전에 나온 러시아 청년 군인에 이르기까지 누가 과연 그 핏값에 책임을 지겠는가?

군사대국 러시아에 맞서 절대 열세의 전력을 가졌던 우크라이나는 비교적 러시아의 침공의도를 정확하게 읽어냈던 미국의 사전 첩보 제공에 따라 전황을 읽는데 도움을 얻고, 야전에서 프론트라인을 형성하기보다 키이우 등지에 시가전을 대비했다.

기갑부대에 주요 전력이 있는 러시아를 상대하기에 개활지가 많은 야전은 우크라이나 전력으로는 상대적으로 불리할 수밖에 없었고, 강대국에게 맞선 시가전 전략은 전투전략 교리로는 당연한 선택지일 수 있겠다. 미국 또한 절대 우위의 일방적 전력을 지니고도 이라크 전쟁, 모술 전투 등 시가전에서 많은 곤욕을 치러보았기에, 러시아 침공에 맞서 우크라이나가 결국 야전에서 주력방어전선을 부대 대 부대로 형성하기에는 열세의 전력으로 밀려날 수밖에 없고, 수도 키이우를 위시한 시가를 배경으로 적을 방어하며 병참을 끊는 등 후방에서 게릴라전을 벌이는 것이 유리한 전략임을 십분 이해했을 공산이 크다. 따라서 미국, 영국, 독일 등 서방이 우크라이나에게 시가전과 기갑전에 대비한 무기와 군수물자를 제공하며 곧 시가전은 우크라이나 정부의 주된 방어 전략 중 하나가 되었다.[31] 그러나 전략상 불가피해보이는 국가적 선택지의 그림자는 곧 무고한 시민사회와 전장을 뒤섞는 일이 된다는 점이다.

또한 상대적으로 러시아는 시리아와 체첸 등지에서 전쟁을 통해 이미 대 시가전에 비교적 익숙한 군대를 보유하거나 굴복시킨 경험이 있다.[32] 러시아는 상대국보다 아무리 우위의 군대를 보유하고 있다하더라도 시가전의 출혈을 잘 알기

---

[31] 미국을 비롯한 서구 주요 국가들은 2014년부터 우크라이나에 30억 달러 이상의 군수물자를 지원해왔으며, 우크라이나 서부 르비우 인근에서 미국 특수 작전 부대가 우크라이나 군을 훈련했다.
https://www.nytimes.com/2022/03/03/us/politics/russia-ukraine-military.html

[32] 스티븐 리 마이어스, 앞의 책(2016), p.205-234.

때문에 시내 내부에 먼저 군대를 본격적으로 진입시키기보다 도시에 융단 폭격이나 포격을 무차별적으로 가함으로써 도시전체가 파괴됨으로 고립무원이 되어 항복, 함락되는 전략을 쓴다.[33] 중세에 성을 에워싼 군대처럼, 성이 곧 도시인 마을에 군인이건 시민이건 피해를 괘념치 않고 통째로 고사시키는 전략을 구사한다.

마리우폴은 물론이거니와 키이우 같은 인구 400만이 살고 있는 대도시는 일찍이 푸틴이 체첸 민족주의자와 이슬람 원리주의자를 분열시켜[34] 시가전에서 많은 출혈을 감수하고도 굴복시킨 전력이 있는 체첸 수도 그로즈니에 비해 몇 배는 큰 도시다. 현대 도시는 옛날 중세의 성채보다 몇 배는 견고한 철근 콘크리트로 지어진 건물들이 즐비하고, 이를 다 포격으로 없애 건물마다 은폐하고 있는 적군을 모조리 드러내자면 러시아의 모든 포탄과 미사일을 사용한다 해도 불능에 가깝다.

---

33 스티븐 리 마이어스, 앞의 책(2016), p.219,228

34 월터 라쿼, 앞의 책(2017), p.290-292.
손영훈, 「체첸-러시아 전쟁의 전개 과정과 국가테러」, 『유라시아 지역의 분쟁』, 민속원, 2014, p.125-130.

따라서 이러한 시가전의 양상은 무고한 시민과 군대가 도시 전선과 전황에 얽혀 함께 죽어갈 수 있다는 점에서 중세 무차별적 야만이 행해지는 공성전만큼 잔인하다.[35] 또 건물 하나마다 곧 중세 성채 하나의 역할을 할 수 있다는 점에서 도시 전체에 전쟁에 사용되는 무기, 폭력의 강도가 과거 야만스러운 중세전쟁의 한 마을이나 도시 함락 작전보다 수천수만 배 이상 크다. 현대전이 과거에 비해 진보하여 정교화되고 고도화되었다고만 누가 말하는가. 현대전은 고대나 중세의 함락과 폭력, 야만과 수치의 총합을 더한 것보다 어떤 의미에서 더욱 냉정하며 잔혹하며 야만적이기까지 하다.

또한 압도적 폭력을 사용할 수 있는 강대국이어서 시가전에서 이기더라도 치러야 할 가공할 출혈을 고려할 때, 도리어 정예지상군 투입, 무차별적 융단 폭격·포격의 소모력에 대한 대가가 상상이상으로 크다. 따라서 도시를 굴복시키기 위해 더 야만적 수단을 동원하려는 유혹을 떨치기가 어렵게 될

---

35 영국 Janes 통계로는 1,2차 체첸 전쟁에서 11,000명의 러시아 군과 체첸 정부군이 사망했다. 그에 반해 체첸 2차 전쟁의 민간인 피해는 최소 8만 명, 체첸 정부는 20만 명, 체첸 반군은 25~30만 명이 사망했다고 추산한다. 최소 기준으로 잡아도 군 피해에 비해 약 8배 가량 민간인 사망자가 발생했다.
손영훈, 앞의 책(2014), p.140.

수 있겠다. 수조원이 넘는 미사일을 쏟아 붓느니, 치명적이나 간단한 화학전을 통한 몰살 유도, 소형 핵탄두의 사용을 통해 재기불능의 타격 등을 도시에 가하는 것이다. 따라서 시가전은 현대에 도시의 규모가 점점 더 메트로폴리스, 거대화되어가는 경향 와중에 전략적 요소로 공방을 불문하고 고려되거나 채택되는 것 자체가 이미 거대한 피와 악을 수반하는 셈이다.

마리우폴은 도시가 시가전의 제물이 되어 이미 수많은 포격·폭격으로 유령화 되었다. 키이우의 시민들은 상당수가 난민이 되었으며, 수도 외곽과 심지어 시가지 내에 아파트, 쇼핑몰까지 포격을 당하며 두려움에 떨고 있다.

이런 잔인한 양상을 실시간으로 목도하면서 세계 시민 사회가 간절히 희망하는 것은 양국의 협상을 통한 휴전과 평화다. 그러나 국제 사회 현실은 그렇게 낭만적이지 않다. 전쟁 상황에서 협정과 휴전이 성립되는 요소는 평화에 대한 국가적 윤리가 작동해서라기보다, 마치 조폭사회와 흡사하게 영역 다툼의 폭력이 이미 착수되어 칼로 낭자히 찌르고 베어 피 흘림이 상당히 차서 집단과 조직에 부담이 될 만큼 임계점이

넘었을 때 협상이나 합의가 성사되는 것과 유사하다.

러시아는 시리아 내전에 익숙해진 자국 시리아 파병 부대를 아직 본격적으로 불러 쓰지도 않았고, 친러화된 - 체첸 전쟁에서 체첸 민족주의자와 이슬람 원리주의자로 분열을 유도해, 반러 체첸군을 궤멸시키고 남은 - 체첸군을 용병으로 삼아 마리우폴에 주력부대 중 하나로 이용하고 있다. 작은 부족이 발전한 민족, 체첸과 10여년에 걸친 장기전을, 푸틴은 질긴 세월동안 관철해 굴복시킨 전력과 자부심이 있다.[36] 우크라이나는 그보다 몇 배나 큰 영토에 수많은 도시를 굴복시켜야만 손에 넣을 수 있다는 소모력이 있지만, 실패해도 크림과 도네츠크, 루한스크를 연결해 얻는 구상만큼은 관철시키고자 전혀 물러서지 않을 것이다. 키이우를 비롯한 우크라이나 전역을 굴복시키고자 한다면 소모력이 문제이고 따라서 화학전, 소형 핵탄두 등 인류 역사 이래로 가장 잔혹하나 소모력에 있어서는 손쉬운 카드도 - 대 세계를 향해 명분이 약하고 악랄할 뿐 - 푸틴은 이미 쥐고 있다. 이것은 어떤 선택이건 간

---

[36] 실제로 푸틴의 지지율도 같은 기간 동안 상승했다. 푸틴이 총리로 임명될 당시(1999.8월)에는 차기 대통령 후보 여론조사에서 2%대의 지지를 받았으나 2차 체첸 전쟁 발발(1999.9월) 이후 10월에는 27%로 급상승했다.
스티븐 리 마이어스, 앞의 책(2016), p.221-223.

에 전쟁이 이미 게시된 이상 막대한 피와 핏값을 담보로 한다.

무고하게 죽어간 자들의 핏값은 도대체 무엇으로 대신할 수 있나. 가족을 잃은 자들의 비탄은 도시는커녕 천지가 뒤집힌 심령이 아니겠나.

그 와중에 도시를 침략당한 우크라이나 시민들의 비폭력 시위는 전시 중 수단과 방법을 가리지 않는 폭력이 집행될 수 있는 군대를 마주하고 중화기를 맨몸으로 막아선 채 일어나고 있다는 점에서 담대하고 용감한 선택이나, 자신과 가족의 피 흘림조차 무릅쓴다는 점에서 슬프고 애달프다. 남은 자들의 슬픔도 슬픔이거니와 전란 중에 졸지에 난민이 되어 타국으로 유랑하듯 쫓겨가 가족과 집을 잃고 언제 돌아오게 될지 모를 본향과 나라를 등져 떠나야 했던 수백만의 난민이 애처롭다.

점점 더 잔혹해져가는 현대전을 소셜 미디어의 발전으로 실시간으로 공유 받거나 목도하는 지금, 우리는 관람평이나 남기는 냉정한 관객이나 되어야겠나? 장기화로 접어들게 되면 될수록 강같이 흐르게 될 무고한 피와 가족과 집을 잃은 수많은 난민들의 벼랑 끝 삶을 목도하며 평화의 사람, 그리스도를 따르는 기독인인 당신과 나는 무엇을 하고 있나? 우리가 선택한 폭력이 아니기에 우리 그리스도인과는 무관한 피인가? 우리는 기도를 통해 천국열쇠를 쥐고 하늘의 주권자 그리스도와 세상을 평화로 맞닿게 하고, 그분의 뜻으로 행전·행동하여 고향과 집, 나라를 잃어버린 난민들을 그분의 사랑과 본향과 그분의 나라로 수렴되도록 섬길 수 있으며, 복음을 통해 세상 왕들과 열국이 흘린 피를 그리스도의 피로 정결케 정화할 수 있음을 우리는 정녕 위급한 이때에 이미 알고 있지 않는가. 이제는 평화를 위해 함께 기도하고 행동할 때이다. 그리스도의 대사들에 평화를 향한 공동행동이 저 잔인한 전선보다 깊어지고 넓어지길 소망해본다.

5 결론
우리의 책무
– 위기와 재앙 사이에서, 전망부재의 기독교인가? 비전의 기독교인가?

기독교 유업이 우크라이나 난민과 전란의 구호를 향해 발빠르게 움직이고 있음을 본다. 기독 선교사들이 전란 중에도 현지인들을 돌보기도하고 인근 국가로 나와 국제사회에 도움과 협력의 루트를 열고 있음의 소식도 종종 들려온다. 세계 위기에 그리스도의 사랑을 품은 기독인들이 공동행동에 있어서 발 빠른 모습을 보이는 것도 아무래도 사실이다. 그러나 한 가지 아쉬운 점이 있다면 이러한 분쟁의 조짐이 이미 10여 년 전 크림반도사태와 도네츠크와 루한스크에 친러 자치정부가 생김으로써[37] 우크라이나 정부와 반목해왔음에도, 대체로 어떤 기독 채널로도 전란의 조짐이나 위기의 상존성(常存性)을 거의 들어본 적이 없다는 점이다.

---

[37] 2014년 4월 루한스크와 도네츠크의 친러 세력은 각각 루간스크 인민공화국(LPR, Луганская Народная Республика), 도네츠크 인민공화국(DPR, Донецкая Народная Республика)으로 분리 독립을 선언했다. 현재 모두 미승인국이다.

기독교는 학문적 전망을 너머 미래 비전의 종교가 아니던가? 하나님은 애굽에 종살이하던 이스라엘의 위기 가운데 백성들의 부르짖음이 찼을 때 바로가 강퍅함으로 해방을 거절, 방해함에도 장자를 치는 단호한 대처를 통해 강퍅함 위에 하나님의 강권을 드러내시고 결국 가나안 땅으로 400여 년 만에 돌아올 것을, 아브라함은 하나님께로부터 비전으로 미리 보고 듣는다.[38] 고레스가 자신의 권세를 위해 지배지역에 세수를 늘리고자 피지배민족의 고토 이주와 그곳의 토착 문화에 따라 정착하기를 장려할 것을 미리 아신 주님께서, 예레미야에게 이스라엘이 바벨론 포로기 이후 70년 만에 고토로 돌아올 것을 미리 비전으로 선포케 하셨다.[39]

선교는 현장을 구원하기 위해 현장을 먼저 이해·연구하는 지역학, R&D 등을 중시했다. 과연 위기를 넘어서 전란에 재앙까지 일어나는 현장은 생명의 막대한 소실과 타격을 받게 된다. 왜 선교사회는 현장 지향적 연구를 부르짖으면서, 동유럽권의 기독전파 관문이자 허브인 우크라이나에 전란을

---

38 창 15:13-14

39 렘 29:10

거의 경고하지 못하였나? 어떤 의미에서는 동유럽 연구를 위한 유학파 자원 못지않게 동유럽, 우크라이나 및 러시아 현장에는 그곳을 이해하고 연구하여 하나님나라로 경영할 수 있는 선교사자원이 상당히 보내어졌음에도, 왜 우리는 우크라이나의 위기를 일말이라도 거의 예보하지 못하였나? 학문도 전망의 역할을 가지며 크림반도 분쟁부터 돈바스 전쟁, 심지어 중국과 대만을 둘러싼 전운 등이 이미 2021년에 이르기까지 계속 연구·보고되거나 경고되어왔다. 그러나 기독교계통에서는 사후약방문처럼 위기가 2022년에 우크라이나 침공을 통해 표면화 되고 나서야 언론 등을 통해 인식 대처되었을 뿐, 위급한 세계적 상황에 대해 기독 R&D연구소나 선교를 위한 국제학, 지역학 연구소 등을 통해 보고된 적이 거의 없다.

더불어 전염병 위기 이후 동유럽권 전란에 연속되어 중국이 대만을 침공하는 일들이 일어난다면, 기독 유업의 침식작용과 함께 대륙을 너머 나가야할 선교 운동의 타격은 매우 심각해질 것이다.

역사 가운데에 서구기독유업이 대륙너머 나아가는 서구 선교운동 전성기 때 1,2차 대전이 일어나 선교운동에 동참, 생명을 살리고자 유럽각지에서 모여 훈련되었던 청년선교사자원들이 도리어 전란에 휘말려 총부리를 들고 서로 죽이며 싸우는 전쟁에 징집된 역사적 교훈을 잊지 않아야한다.

시진핑의 공언대로 만약 중국까지 대만을 침공한다면 아시아 비서구권 기독교가 성장하고 팽창 성숙해가는 와중에 한반도를 비롯한 아시아 선교운동에 결정적 타격으로 작용할 것이다.

다시 경고하건대, 시진핑은 베이징 동계 올림픽 어간 우크라이나 침공계획을 푸틴 측에게 먼저 듣고 가을에 대만 침공을 푸틴에게 상호적으로 밝혔다. 중국의 대만 침공이 기정사실화 되면, 미국과 일본의 대만해협 확보를 인한 전쟁 개입을 염두에 두고도, 시진핑은 대만과 중국 사이 분쟁은 같은 민족 상의 내정 갈등과 내전일 뿐이라며 국제사회의 개입에 부담을 주려는 명분을 만들 것이다.[40] 이미 서구를 비롯해 중국과 수교를 맺은 나라들은 대만을 국가로 인정하지 않는다는 표명을 전제로 중국과 수교를 맺기도 했다. 따라서 푸틴처럼 이해관계가 맞는다면 시진핑은 국제사회의 반발을 알고도 내

---

40 공민석, 앞의 책(2019), p.81.

부적, 외부적으로 전쟁 명분을 만들 수 있음을 유의해야한다. 그럼에도 바로와 고레스의 마음처럼 푸틴과 시진핑의 마음을 다스리고 그들의 이해관계와 욕망 등의 선택지 위에서 사람의 마음과 나라와 세계에 역사하는 분은 주님이시다. 또한 믿음의 사람들에게 비전과 시대적 경고를 알리시고 위기와 재앙사이에서 파국을 돌이키게 하시기도 하신다.

설령 중국이 러시아에 이어 연속적으로 전쟁을 선택한다 해도 믿음의 사람들에 기도와 평화를 향한 협력, 전란에 휩쓸린 사람들에 대한 구호, 국제사회의 조정 등으로 다시 악을 선으로 바꾸실 분도 주님이시다. 그러나 전염병과 유라시아 서구와 동아시아 간 전쟁의 연속으로 생명보다 사망이 창궐하는 역사를 속수무책으로 그냥 마주하기에는 그 파국과 파괴가 매우 심각할 것이 자명하다. 전망하고 경고해 전쟁과 재앙 파국을 막는 그리스도인들의 기도를 먼저 결집시켜야한다.

러시아에 이어 중국조차 전쟁을 선택한다면 말할 것 없이 대만, 미국, 일본, 러시아, 북한, 대한민국 등 동아시아를 중심으로 다시 한 번 직간접적 세계대전이 일어나 저주에 가깝게 느껴지는 재앙이 임하게 될 것이다. 여기에서 패거리 전쟁에 휩쓸리지 않고자 중립국 선언 등의 구상도, 국제사회에 냉혹한 힘의 논리와 역학관계의 현실을 직시할 때는 나이브하고 순진한 대책이 될 것이 자명해 보인다. 국제질서는 한반도, 대한민국은 물론이거니와 북한까지 분명 한편에서 전쟁에 가담할 것을 강력으로 요구 관철하려 할 것이다. 중국은 미국의 패권에서 벗어나는 도전을 이미 오래전에 구상 시행하고 있고, 미국은 중국과 맞설 대처를 이미 기민하게 준비해 국력의 상당부분을 그 대결에 압도를 위해 오래전부터 용수철처럼 압축해 조여 놓았다.(2021년 어간이 아니어도 중국과 미국은 우리 시대에 구조적으로 부딪칠 공산이 크다.)[41] 전쟁이 개시된다면 서구의 기독 유업의 정체나 후퇴가운데 한반도를 비롯한 비서구 동아시아 기독교도 전란과 그 후유증으로 상당히 침식되거나 표류할 것이 자명하다.[42]

따라서 이런 위기의 전조를 전망·인지하면서도 그 경고를 무시하고, 믿는 자들조차 전망 없이 시대가 그냥 흘러가리라

---

41 공민석, 앞의 책(2019), p.108.
42 2008년 1월, 미국의 비영리연구기관 랜드연구소의 보고서는 대만문제를 놓고 미중 간 무력 충돌이 발생하게 될 경우, 미군의 접근 저지를 위한 중국군의 선제 기습 공격 대상 중에 한국의 오산과 군산을 포함하고 있다.
조용성, 앞의 책(2012), p.112.

는 역사의식은 위험하고 무책임하다. 위기가 재앙과 파국이 되기 전에 시대 앞에 경고하고 돌이키도록 기도하여 주님께서 악을 막아주시도록 청원하며, 일어난 악에 관해서는 연대된 공동행동으로 전란 중에 구호 등을 통해 난민과 환란당한 나라를 섬길 필요가 있다.

또한 이번뿐만 아니라, 전란의 소문과 전란은 항상 국가 사이에 있을 찐데 세상 나라보다 더 큰 하나님나라의 비전을, 세계와 시대를 넘어선 복음의 평화와 소망의 비전을, 세계에 전개해야할 책임이 그리스도인들에게 끝날까지 반드시 있다.

6 함께 할 기도방향

1) 러시아와 중국이 선택하거나 선택할 수 있는 확전과 전쟁의 위협을 주님 손 안에서 막아주시고, 믿는 자들의 기도가 들불처럼 일어나 바로와 고레스의 생각을 주관하신 주님께서 푸틴과 시진핑을 비롯한 위정자들의 마음에 재앙과 파국의 선택을 돌이키게 하소서

2) 동유럽권 우크라이나 등지에 선교사님들과 크리스천들이 일어나 한국교회, 세계교회와 함께 우크라이나 난민과 전란 중에 있는 자들을 섬기며 하나님나라가 사랑과 평화, 위로의 본향이 됨을 섬김을 통해 나타나게 하소서

3) 세계가 전염병, 전쟁 등의 위기를 통과하며 기독선교유업이 침식과 침륜을 경험하는 가운데서도 주의 등불이 꺼지지 않아 어둠을 향해 예수의 빛을 비추며, 세계를 영광으로 돌이킬 추수할 일꾼을 일으키고 보내소서

4) 세계 나라와 국제질서 너머 일하시고 역사하는 공의와 사랑, 평강의 하나님나라가 속히 모든 나라와 민족 가운데 선

포되고 역사되어 하나님나라가 완성되고 영원한 샬롬, 평화가 온 세계에 이루어지게 하소서

참고도서 및 참조정보

가오샤오, 『대륙의 리더 시진핑(새로운 중국의 지도자 시진핑 그의 삶을 통해 본 중국의 현대사)』, 하진이 옮김, 삼호미디어(2012)

공민석, 『미중 갈등의 구조(금융 위기 이후의 헤게모니 경쟁, 북 저널리즘)』, 스리체어스(2019).

글로벌협력본부, 『디지털로 바라본 우크라이나-러시아 사태』, 한국지능정보사회진흥원(2022),

김성진, 「몰도바-트랜스드니에스트리아 분쟁의 배경과 전개」, 『유라시아 지역의 분쟁』, 민속원 (2014), 45-77쪽.

니얼 퍼거슨, 『둠 재앙의 정치학 (전 지구적 재앙은 인류에게 무엇을 남기는가)』, 홍기빈 옮김, 21세기북스(2021).

마르가레타 몸젠, 『푸틴 신디케이트 (비밀경찰수중에 놓인 러시아)』, 이윤주 옮김, 한울(2019).

베네딕트 앤더슨, 『상상의 공동체 (민족주의의 기원과 전파에 대한 성찰)』, 윤형숙 옮김, 나남(2004).

손상호, 「금융혁신 8대 과제」, 한국금융연구원, 2022.

손영훈, 「체첸-러시아 전쟁의 전개과정과 국가테러」, 『유라시아 지역의 분쟁』, 민속원, 2014, 117.

스티븐 리 마이어스, 『뉴차르 (블라디미르 푸틴 평전)』, 이기동 옮김, 프리뷰(2016).

아자 가트, 알렉산더 야콥슨, 『민족 (정치적 종족성과 민족주의, 그 오랜 역사와 깊은 뿌리)』, 유나영 옮김, 교유서가(2020).

에릭 홉스봄, 사라 모 건, 『만들어진 전통』, 박지향 옮김, 휴머니스트(2004).

에릭 홉스봄, 『1780년 이후의 민족과 민족주의 (창비신서 125)』, 강명세 옮김, 창작과비평사(1998).

월터 라쿼, 『푸티니즘 (푸틴 열풍과 폭주하는 러시아)』, 김성균 옮김, 바다출판사(2017).

이근욱, 『아프가니스탄 전쟁』, 한울아카데미(2021),

장병옥, 「체첸-러시아 갈등의 역사에 관한 연구 - 체첸의 이슬람 세력화를 중심으로」, 『국제지역연구』, 13(1), 국제지역학회, 2009, 513-530.

정세진, 『러시아 이슬람 (역사·이념·전쟁)』, 민속원(2014).

정세진, 「체첸 민족의 정체성 형성에 관한 소고」, 『러시아어문학연구논집』 44집(2013), 한국러시아문학회, 507-537쪽.

정세진, 「체첸 전쟁의 기원: 러시아와 체첸의 역사적 갈등관계를 중심으로」, 『슬라브학보』, 20(2), 한국슬라브유라시아학회, 2005, 355-386.

제라르 샬리앙, 소피 무세, 『쿠르드 연대기 (IS 시대의 쿠르드족 문제)』, 은정 펠스너 옮김, 한울(2018).

조성훈 선임연구위원, 「빅테크에 대한 공정경쟁 규제 동향 및 금융산업 진출 관련 이슈」, 『자본시장포커스』, 2022-06호, 자본시장연구원.

조용성, 『중국의 미래 10년』, 넥서스BIZ(2012).

조지 프리드먼, 『다가오는 유럽의 위기와 지정학 (브렉시트, 유럽연합의 와해 그리고 독일 문제의 재부상)』, 홍지수 옮김, 김앤김북스(2020).

탁양현, 『러시아 역사, 키예프 루스 모스크바 공국 러시아 제국 소련 연방 러시아 연방』, e퍼플(2020).

파스칼 보니파스, 『지정학 지금 세계에 무슨 일이 벌어지고 있는가?』, 최린 옮김, 가디언(2019).

한스 페터 마르틴, 『게임 오버』, 이지윤 옮김, 한빛비즈(2020).

한양대 아태지역연구센터 러시아 유라시아 연구사업단, 『유라시아 지역의 국가, 민족 정체성』, 한울아카데미(2010).

한양대학교 아태지역연구센터 러시아 유라시아 연구사업단, 『유라시아 지역의 분쟁』, 민속원(2014).

현승수, 「러시아연방 북캅카스 지역의 테러와 분쟁 확대」, 『유라시아 지역의 분쟁』, 민속원(2014), 79-115쪽.

홍완석, 「험난한 여정, 러시아의 체첸분쟁: 원인과 경과, 그리고 전망」, 『한국정치학회보』, 39(5), 한국정치학회, 2005, 237-262.

KBS 다큐 인사이트 팬데믹 머니 제작팀, 『팬데믹 머니』, 리더스북(2021).

Bains, P., Sugimoto, N., Wilson, C., 2022, 「Big Tech in financial services: Regulatory approaches and architecture」, Fintech note 2022/002, IMF.

Boissay, F., Ehlers, T., Gambacorta, L., Shin, H.S., 2021, 「Big techs in finance: on the new nexus between data privacy and competition」, BIS working papes No.970.

Carstens, A., Claessens, S., Restoy, F., Shin, H.S., 2021, 「Regulating big techs in finance」, BIS Bulletin No.45.

Crisanto, J.C., Ehrentraud, J., Lawson, A., Restoy, F., 2021, 「Big tech regulations: what is going on?」, FSI insights on policy implementation No.36, BIS.

Shin, H.S., 2019, 「Big tech in finance: opportunities and risks」, BIS Annual Economic Report.

림바흐, 레이몬드. "스탈린그라드 전투". 브리태니커 백과사전, 2021년 8월 15일, https://www.britannica.com/event/Battle-of-Stalingrad. 2022년 4월 6일에 액세스함.

Historian Niall Ferguson Predicts the Future of China.
https://youtu.be/IIApVciCScw 2022.2.27.

Yuval Noah Harari, 「Why Vladimir Putin has already lost this war」, 『The Guardian Weekly』, 2022.03.28., https://www.theguardian.com/commentisfree/2022/feb/28/vladimir-putin-war-russia-ukraine

https://www.bbc.com/ukrainian/news-60583913

https://www.nytimes.com/2022/03/03/us/politics/russia-ukraine-military.html

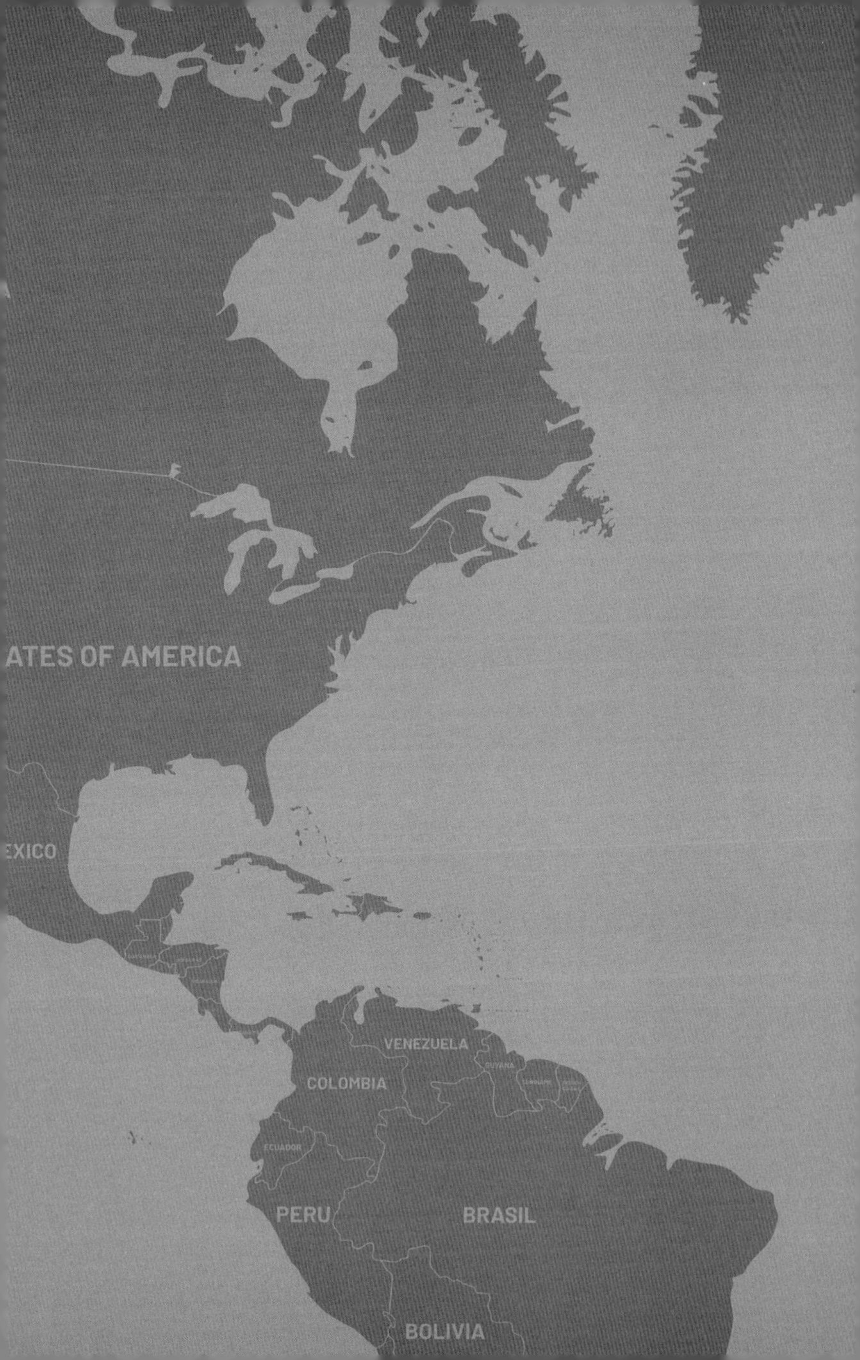
ATES OF AMERICA
EXICO
VENEZUELA
GUYANA
COLOMBIA
ECUADOR
PERU
BRASIL
BOLIVIA

Opinions on
Ukraine and the World

우크라이나와 세계를
바라보며

Notice

This article was written around March 2022.

I would like to inform you that the introduction has started to be written in the form of a column for the column contribution to 『Mission Times』.

Preface

There are several reasons why I rushed to write an opinion about Ukraine in an urgent situation, even though I knew it would become a poor book.

There is a small people group we have been cherishing and praying for 20 years in the Crimean peninsula, which had already become a sign of conflict between Ukraine and Russia several years ago. The people who had believed in Islam for a long time and were taken to Central Asia as about two-thirds of the population died due to Stalin's forced migration, returned to Crimea around 2000, when they were forgotten even by scholars of international studies and regional studies and thought to be extinct. The existence of the nation was proved by their indomitable viability.

Even though their ethnic religion was Islam when they returned to the Christian country of Ukraine and were placed in an environment where they could hear the gospel without restrictions, there were hardly any studies about them or opinions to inform the international community of their identity. From my youth when I had a missionary vision in my 20s, the continuous heart of prayer meeting for them has become the core spirit of the Vision Mission that I pioneered until today. Our prayers were meaningful, so we continued to send scouting and pioneering teams to them, found they have been close to the Korean diaspora in Russia, and confirmed the locals who accepted the gospel through short-term mission teams. While praying for this people group(who never heard the gospel for 2000years) for the past 20years, we found the possibility of being evangelized through contact with long-term missionaries if they are connected with Pentecostal background Ukrainian local church that has revival.

So while this booklet tries to write an objective perspective in front of the global timeliness of the invasion of Ukraine, in fact, personally the intention of self-criticism and repentance is at the bottom. I have been proclaiming that the lost ethnic groups for over 2,000years will return to the Lord and have salvation and peace if two or three people gather to pray and act in the gospel. So it contains sorrow and reflection as to whether the Crimean Peninsula and entire Ukraine were handed over to a war of conflict and slaughter due to the lack of awareness of the times.

Therefore, as I am a missionary, wrote to the best of my poor ability for the world to return to the kingdom of God and to have the progress of His gospel and peace through people of faith, before the world is further engulfed in darkness due to the structural conflict between the great powers surrounding Russia, China, and the US.

As stated in the body of the text, I hope this booklet will serve as a small flashpoint that sparks prayer and gospel act, Christian's common action and service, and Christ's ambassador of peace for the world swept away by pandemics and wars.

Therefore, this booklet will be distributed by young people like the dew of dawn in the direction of continuously triggering like a small wave, such as joint solidarity, movement, and service physically and spiritually. Even small waves gather and continue to ripple, and the ocean moves.

This article was also started with a request to contribute to a column in 『Mission Times』. Since it was an article that contained urgent issues to deal with in a timely manner, the draft was also segmented and sent out on social media, but the small column became a longer article and larger booklet due to the staff's mistake of checking the amount of the column. The Lord who makes even mistakes work together for the good, will awaken our hearts again and make us walk with Christ through the awakening of the Holy Spirit, who leads us to sense these successive crises if we have a responsibility we have missed toward the times and world.

31. Mar. 2022 Missionary David Cho

Thanks to

Thanks for all advanced of faith who was being inspiration of nourish- ment and also I thank you all staff Kyoungeun Yu, Hyeji Park who helped proofreading and editing, and staff Hyeog-gi Gwon who did graceful design, and staff Siwon Park, Haeun Ban, Eunhye Son who did translation, and about 350 mission staffs who works together in Vision Mission community.

My family a wife and Eunbit, Sihoo and Annyeong are my treasures who never reject the community lifestyle to live with the word of God. Of course the Lord will pick up the torch of His word to light dark age beside us, but that is why I am really appreciate His word is with us.

1 Introduction
- Post Pandemic, and the war

British scholar Niall Ferguson, a professor at Harvard University, predicted that global catastrophe and crisis after the pandemic would be a war in 『Doom: The Politics of Catastrophe』, which describes the course of the global pandemic from the beginning to middle period. In 2021, this prediction was not only Niall Ferguson's opinion but simultaneously emerged as a common perspective or issue of the times by many scholars.

He cautiously but firmly predicted a world war between civilizations centered on tensions between China and Taiwan, which is going beyond all-out wars between nations, because of cracks in unilateral hegemony or relatively misjudgment of hegemonic competition between major powers such as the US, China, and Russia after the pandemic.[1]

---

[1] Chapter 11 and the conclusion deal with issues between the US and China, mentioning that 'new cold war' and 'geopolitical disaster'. Niall Ferguson, 『Doom: The Politics of Catastrophe』, Penguin Press, 2021.

The international community is worrying that the Russian-Ukraine war could become a destructive world war between several countries and civilizations, beyond an all-out war between two countries.[2] Therefore, anxiety rises because of the prediction of global catastrophe, the war following the pandemic that Prof. Ferguson's forecasts of the times seem to have crossed the half-line.

The mainstream conflict between the world, predicted by Niall Ferguson, is tension between the US and China, while partially acknowledging the gap between the US and Russia – which also includes China as a central conflict.[3]

As if corroborating his prediction, Chinese President Xi Jinping declared that he would definitely solve the Taiwan issue within his term as he seeks to reign power again for the third term. Looking at the Russia-Ukraine war, Taiwanese President

---

[2] Hans-Peter Martin, 『Game Over – Wohlstand fur wenige, Demokratie fur niemand, Nationalismus fur alle – und dann?』, Penguin Verlag Munchen, 2018, p.433-436.

[3] Historian Niall Ferguson Predicts the Future of China. https://youtu.be/IlApVciCScw 2022.2.27.

Tsai Ing-wen said that China is also threatening and dividing Taiwan, just like the invasion of Russia, and ordered readiness condition to the entire army. And the slogan "After Ukraine, Taiwan is next." spread throughout Taiwanese civil society with their concern.

If the Russia-Ukraine war is prolonged or if neighboring Moldova, Georgia, Syria, Chechnya, Belarus, Poland, and Lithuania are drifted into direct or indirect war, there is anxiety that even Europe or the Americas may join the war where Western Christian heritage has existed for a long time.[4] What should we Christians and ministers do if that happens?

If the conflict around Taiwan between China and the US turns on the surface and escalates into international tension or war, which Niall Ferguson noticed, then there is a strong pos-

---

4 In the name of the annexation of Crimea in 2014, Putin advocated the 'protection of the same race'. Several NATO member countries have regions with large Russian populations.
Steven Lee Myers, 「The New Tsar: The Rise and Reign of Vladimir Putin」, Vintage Books USA, 2016.

sibility that South Korea, North Korea Japan, and Russia will be drifted into the war directly or indirectly by a tripwire. What should we Christians and missionaries who look at the world prepare for the future while we are looking at the epidemic in the front and the tension of shadowy war from the back?

△ Picture 1 **The Flag of Ukraine**

2 Putinism, Xi Jinping, Shi Huangdi^(Ancient Chinese Emperor) and Nero

The modern state has a more complex system than in ancient times, and various factors are considered when decisions are made. It also goes the same with deciding to wage war between countries.

Nevertheless, the forecast of whether Russia and China will either escalate or adhere/choose war could be speculated through a few narrowed-down key factors.

This is because both countries are ruled by oligarchy or dictatorship (even though they are modern states) in which decision-making depends on a few powers.

Both countries inherited the one-party communist dictatorship. Not to mention that these countries are at the peak of the hierarchical and pyramid structure, in which the power is monopolized by a few or arbitrary individuals, as opposed to the collective leadership system.[5]

---

[5] Margareta Mommsen, 『Das Putin-Syndikat (Russland im Griff der Geheimdienstler)』, C.H.Beck, 2017. p.6-7.

△ Picture 2 **Pray for Ukraine**

Russia and China are modern countries and advocated a republic or collective leadership system. However, just like autocratic emperors Nero and Domitian emerged in the Roman Republic, Russia has built a long-running dictatorship while being a Republic, so-called 'Putinism'. This dictatorship was based on a network of minority elite politicians, soldiers, and monopolistic entrepreneurs led by Putin, with a KGB background.[6]

---

[6] It is defined as a state capitalist dictatorship.
Walter Laqueur, 『Putinism: Russia and Its Future with the West』, Thomas Dunne Books, 2015. p.245.

Also, in China, where Xi Jinping was also the son of a high-ranked bureaucrat who had been expelled to the outskirts, but with his unique prudent decisions, he rose to the presidency, the top of the oligarchy of the Communist Party of China. He built the foundation of a one-man dictatorship by suppressing and keeping an eye on other key oligarchies under the name of eradicating corruption. He even passed the Constitutional Amendment Bill of the National People's Congress of China about extending his power after two consecutive terms in office.

Xi Jinping opened the door to a third term in power, which seems like he could hold a life-long tenure. It is now common among experts to nickname Xi Jinping "the Emperor of Shi Huang," rather than the president of the country.

Many scholars are focusing on the forecasts and arguments that there are some elements for them to start, continue, or expand war while they have built up monopoly power.

Nevertheless, it would be better for us Christians to use the biblical viewpoint (analogic) as the standard of how God viewed Emperor Nero.

Paul encouraged the readers in the book of Romans (13:1) to obey the rulers. The period that Paul wrote this book was around AD 58. Ironically, this was during Nero's reign. Also around AD 65, 1 Timothy was written. The book tells the readers to pray for kings and those in high positions, This era was when Nero's tyranny was running towards its peak.

This is an encouragement to accept Emperor Nero's authority and to pray for him, who will act against God's will and destroy the world and Christianity with evil. Without faith in the Sovereign Lord, who gave authority over all powers and will integrate all authorities into the kingdom of God, this was an attitude and prayer that was impossible for Christians at that time.

Having a neurosis, Nero pursued populism and feared the rejection of people so he even killed his mother himself to be in power. He treated those who were under him recklessly, causing him to promote arson against his citizens and frame Christians for it. Before all this happened, God wanted Christians to pray to the Lord so Nero could change his evil decisions. This encouragement for Christians at that time to pray for Nero may be quite incomprehensible. However, the Lord gave Nero an opportunity to revise his decisions just before an evil choice or tyranny. Just before AD 100 years, God surely judged Nero as 666 for choosing evil in the book of Revelation. History always remembered him as the one who chose evil and evaluated him for generations. This represents God's judgment and justice.

Through this article, I will analyze modern Putinism and the Shi Huangdi system. However, the future is unknown whether the war will escalate and continue, or whether there will be an all-out war between other countries or a world war between civilizations. It is necessary to pray for systems that are about to make evil choices or international situations. However, I will analyze the tempting factors that could trigger Putin and Xi Jinping to choose war or escalation. In addition, it is very urgent for the saints, who are in contact with the Lord's sovereignty, to pray with one heart before they choose the trigger of evil. They will make their own choices. However, considering the pain of world citizens and people that their decisions will inflict, and the amount of evil that hasn't been chosen, and is yet to be unfolded, the divine burden of our prayers must rather be huge now. Now is a critical time to pray for the world.

1) Possibility of war progression in Ukraine under Putinism

It is true that after the collapse of the Soviet Union, Putin's long-term dictatorship continued the culture of communism's confidential authoritarian structure, due to Putin's KGB background in the Soviet Union. However, "Putinism" is not a single-component dictatorship like the former Soviet Union.

Putin is inevitably at the top (due to the post-totalitarian system) among elites from the Secret Service, bureaucrats, and monopoly entrepreneurs who are protected and supported by the government. However, the key to his long-term dictatorship and the revival of his regime was based on populism.[7]

---

[7] Margareta Mommsen, same as the previous book(2017), p.85,104.

Putin appealed to the desire of the Russian public, who wanted to restore the status of a world power again after the collapse of the Soviet Union, He revived Russia's economic power (which had collapsed after the Soviet Union) through the export and development of energy resources. On this basis, the legitimacy of his long-term dictatorship was established.[8] Therefore, it would not totally be a propaganda that the media report of Putin's approval rate is still over 65% even with the invasion of Ukraine.

---

[8] The period of Putin's rule is applied to the petrostate(a compound word of petroleum + state, which refers to countries with a form of power that monopolized by accumulates significant capital from oil-producing countries or petroleum and natural gas).
Walter Laqueur, same as the previous book(2017), p.400-403.

△ Picture 3 **Russian President Vladimir Putin(Влади́мир Пу́тин)**

Therefore the West's anticipation or aspiration that "Putinism" could be overthrown by Putin completely exhausting Russia's national power through this unreasonable war and facing difficulties such as international restrictions, maybe the West's bias. There is an aspect that during the pandemic, the western society (which was divided due to the quarantine policies of personal freedom versus public hygiene) was united temporarily by putting restrictions on Russia.

However, it is also true that more than half of the world did not participate in the restrictions because China, India, the Middle East, and many countries in South America did not participate.

Also, even if Putin is removed, the crowd would still long for another powerful leader to replace Putin, who catered to the Russian people's desire. It is likely that elites and alternative figures, who have learned a similar dictatorship culture around Putin, will emerge.

Of course, Putin experienced fierce resistance from the Ukrainian people at the beginning of the war during the beginning stage of the Ukraine invasion. So they are fighting the war of attrition and have yet achieved their goal of establishing a pro-Russian puppet government. However, the expectation, that Russia(The world's second-largest military and energy power) will lose in the beginning stage of war due to these attritions and lack of power and logistics, maybe a hasty prediction of the current situation.

Ukraine is indeed the largest country in Europe (except Russia), and they led the war to a war of attrition with their will of resistance. However, even though Russia failed to draw out the breakdown of the Ukrainian government in the first stage of the war, it continues to fight according to the tactics it has always been using.

The way that Russia secures influence in Georgia, Syria, Chechnya, Moldova, Lithuania, and Belarus is similar or almost identical to the attrition warfare in the current Ukraine war.[9] First, Russia stations pro-Russian units or Russian troops around and in parts of the territory. If it sees resistance, it draws out civil war or even dares to start a war through the troops already stationed and divide the country. Finally, it establishes a satellite government approved by the Russian government or a pro-Russian autonomous republic.

---

9 Hanyang University Asia Pacific Research Center Russia Eurasia Research Group, 「Eurasia's national and ethnic identity」, Hanul Academy, 2010, p.185, 224–225.

Russia has expanded its influence of violence, which was already practiced in smaller autonomous principalities and minor states, which the West knew but ignored or didn't intervene. In Ukraine, which is larger and closer to the west, Russia is already practicing and unfolding its strategy of division, overthrow, and satellite domination.[10]

In addition, Russia is already carrying out these strategies consistently. Russia is besieging and indiscriminately bombing entire cities such as Mariupol, which connects the Crimean Peninsula in southern Ukraine, Lugansk, and Donetsk in eastern Ukraine, and even citizens are depleted of water and food. Russia creates isolation where access is difficult and ultimately draws out submission.

After that, Russia replaces the mayor with pro-Russian personnel and is practicing violence (even under the current war of attrition, which was only delayed due to unexpectedly fierce resistance) and division, reorganizing southern and eastern

---

[10] George Friedman, 『Flashpoints: The Emerging Crisis in Europe』, Anchor Books, 2016, p.210.

Ukraine into the pro-Russian territory. Therefore, we should not jump to conclusions and make predictions or propaganda that Russia's invasion and the influence of physical violence will easily fail. The purpose and intentions of the physical violence by Putin and Russia's invasion of Ukraine have already damaged Ukraine and are not easily subdued, so they are achieving half of their intended purpose.

△ Picture 4 **The military situation of Russia's invasion in Ukraine**

But even if Putin is half successful in warfare and physical invasion, it is likely that Putin and Russia will be almost completely defeated in intellectual history. In other words, "Putinism", which longs for the Russian influence of the past, may achieve its intended goal in the battle of physical violence. However, in intellectual history, we can't help but think that Russia is falling into a pit of major defeat or failure.

Yuval Noah Harari[11], a professor at the Hebrew University views Russia as following the footsteps of the German army. Germany was on a winning streak until it fought in Stalingrad (Russia) in World War II and was defeated.

The background that led to the golden age of Russia and the Soviet Union, was not because the communist system functioned well without contradictions. It was rather based on the story of Russia's historical victory over Germany. It started as Russia being cornered by the world-power Germany and even letting them enter Stalingrad and destroying the entire city, but

---

11 Yuval Noah Harari, 「Why Vladimir Putin has already lost this war」, 『The Guardian Weekly』, 2022.03.28., https://www.theguardian.com/commentisfree/2022/feb/28/vladimir-putin-war-russia-ukraine

not giving up on resistance and street fights and finally making the Germans retreat.[12]

Ironically, even though this invasion exposed Ukraine's southeast and northern parts to Russia's unilateral invasion and violence, their persistent resistance against the great power of Russia, will be the fundamental spirit of Ukraine.

As noted by the scholar Eric Hobsbawm, due to the characteristics of the modern nation[13], people unite according to mythology and the common vision of citizens. Ukrainian's national spirit, which is persistently resisting Russia, can further strengthen the national mentality of Ukrainians in intellectual history.

---

[12] The Russians consider it to be one of the greatest battles of thief Great Patriotic War, and most historians consider it to be the greatest battle of the entire conflict.
Limbach, Raymond. "Battle of Stalingrad". Encyclopedia Britannica, 15 Aug. 2021, https://www.britannica.com/event/Battle-of-Stalingrad. Accessed 6 April 2022.

[13] E. J. Hobsbawm, 「Nations and Nationalism since 1780」, Cambridge University Press, 2012. p.68
Benedict R. O'G. Anderson, 「Imagined Communities: Reflections on the Origin and Spread of Nationalism」, 1983. p.25

Even if Russia exerts its full force in terms of physical violence to pressure Ukraine, violence damages and occupies Ukrainian cities, Ukraine is asymmetrically oppressed, there seems to be a high possibility of Ukraine overpowering and winning over "Putinism" and Russia in terms of long-term intellectual history.

2) Is Xi Jinping trying to make Taiwan as his scapegoat to become Emperor Shi Huangdi?
- Analysis of Xi Jinping's possibility of waging war following Putin

After the fall of the Soviet Union, Putin assumed Russia's identity as if they are Europe (Eastern Rome) and used a friendly diplomatic approach to the EU and NATO in the early days of his rule. Following President Yeltsin, he even showed a diplomatic stance to join forces with the West by allowing Russia to enter NATO and the EU.[14] However, after the second half of his reign, Putin began to separate from the West and build their own identity historically. He tried to find the identity of Russia in the historicity of the Eurasia continent rather than in the affinity with western Europe. One of the reasons was the West's crucial mistake of pride.

Due to Putin's Western-friendly attitude in the early days of his rule, NATO and the EU's key countries generally viewed Russia as a downgraded successor of the collapsed Soviet Union. With this mindset, the United States and the West diplomatically treated Russia as a fallen Soviet Union. This inhospitality was hard to tolerate for Putin, who had dreamed his way to reaching the world's second-largest military power and even economic revival. After that, Putin still emphasized that Russia is the successor of the Eastern Roman Empire using the Russian Orthodox Church. However, after the second half of his regime, Putin set up a historical distinction from the West and built Russia's own identity from the Eurasian continent (which

---

14 Margareta Mommsen, same as the previous book(2017), p.153-154.

connects Russia and Asia), rather than from affinity with the West (western Rome), including the Americas and Europe.[15]

It is no exaggeration to say that this attitude opened up the stance of prudent Xi Jinping towards the Chinese dream and the G1's world power, even risking tensions and international conflicts. Following manmandi (Chinese word for 'slow action or slow progress') spirit, China has a strong approach to strategic hegemony, not revealing its aggressive claws until China becomes a dominant country.[16] Also, China has been careful of its one-on-one tension with the United States to not stand out before China dominates hegemony. Nevertheless, the Asian(China) perspective on understanding the world elements of conflict, tension, and competition is more skillful at understanding tripartite competition (such as a game of rock scissor paper) than the one-on-one bilateral confrontation of the Western perspective.

---

15 From the beginning, the West pursued an anti-Russian policy and sought to transform Russia into semi colonial dependent on the West technologically and economically.
Walter Laqueur, same as the previous book(2015), p.375–376.

16 Hans-Peter Martin, same as the previous book(2018), p.138–152.

Putin and Russia had relatively pro-Western policies in the early days of their rule, as members of actual international politics. However, the West did not actively embrace and respect Putin and Russia and lost them due to confrontation. This opened an opportunity for Xi Jinping (and China) to approach a three-way confrontation between the United States versus China and Russia, rather than viewing the conflict of hegemony between the United States versus China only. Previously through the Syrian Civil War, Russia provided military aid to the Shiite al-Assad dictatorship and government forces while the United States supported Sunni Free-Syrian rebels. This strengthened the dictatorship within Syria and established Islamic extremist systems in the Middle East such as Daesh and ISIS, which stemmed and given opportunities from the Sunni Free-Syrian rebels supported by the United States. [17]

Whether the United States was intentional or ignorant,

---

[17] Gérard Chaliand, Sophie Mousset, 「Question kurde : à l'heure de Daech」, Hanul, 2018. p.152.

ISIS emerged from the Sunni rebels, supported by the United States, and expanded its influence. ISIS has phenomenally ruined China's dream of opening trade routes in the Middle East[18] (Belt and Road Initiative)[19]. As ISIS settled near the borders of Turkey, Syria, and Iran, where Kurdish people live, China's ambitious dream of trade route in the Middle East was bottleneck-jammed or even blocked due to system turmoil and the rise of Islamic extremism.[20]

The withdrawal of the US from Afghanistan is also a byproduct of the result for the US trying to focus on the competition with China, considering China as its main enemy. The United States was well aware of the pervasive corruption of the Afghan

---

18 The One Belt, One Road project is a large-scale civil engineering project. It will connect Europe and Africa beyond East and South Asia and Central Asia by land and seaway, and build roads, ports, railways, and industrial complexes to aim to build the economic circle of 65 neighboring countries by 2030.

19 KBS Documentary Insight Pandemic Money Production Team, 『Pandemic money』, Readers book, 2021, p.217.

20 Gérard Chaliand, Sophie Mousset, same as the previous book(2018), p.168-169.

self-government that it could not even stand on its own. It was also quite predictable that the Taliban would overthrow the autonomous government and take over the system if the US forces withdrew from such incompetent Afghan self-government.[21] However, there is even a view that the US deliberately abandoned US military weapons that could fall into the hands of the Taliban and made a clumsy withdrawal. The mysterious reason why the United States withdrew its troops from Afghanistan while leaving a lot of US military equipment in Afghanistan is because of the prospect that if the Xinjiang, Uyghurs, etc, in western China become the stage for extremist Islamist activities, it becomes a tool for the United States to keep an eye on China through collaborating and connecting with the Taliban.

There is also a view that the cause of Saddam Hussein's fall from being pressured through the Iraq War was the US' revenge for Hussein's bold attempt to challenge US hegemony by trading oil in currencies other than dollars. Similarly, Xi Jinping has already specifically conducted and established a trade route

---

[21] Geun-wook Lee, 『War in Afghanistan』, Hanul Academy, 2021, p.405, 425.

with oil-producing countries that trade in RMB (Chinese currency) rather than dollars.[22]

The Chinese dream that Xi Jinping had foreseen towards the international community is also likely to end in an empty dream. Some prospects that China's hegemony will outpace the United States after the 2030s have dimmed. China's national power to rise to the G1 or achievement of the global international agenda has largely been lost due to the retreat or delay of the Belt and Road Initiative, the accumulation of contradictions between government and shadow finance within China, and the failure to build a huge ghost town for propagating its economic boom, etc.

China and Xi Jinping are aware that the elements of conflict and tension in the competition for hegemony with the United States are ripening to an unavoidable degree externally and

---

[22] KBS Documentary Insight Pandemic Money Production Team, same as the previous book(2021), p.224..

internationally.[23] Also, they are experiencing difficulties and exhaustion in setting the global agenda they have advocated. Therefore, under this real international political situation, Niall Ferguson predicts the increasing possibility of Xi Jinping establishing a Chinese identity by emphasizing the elements of internal nationalism to establish legitimacy for the third term in power and national unity.[24]

In other words, Xi Jinping is considering the possibility of resetting the old conflict with Taiwan, that is, trying to carry the viewpoint internationally that both sides are one China. It would be difficult for prudent Xi Jinping to confront the United States alone or with China's manmandi mentality. However, conflicts and collisions are inevitable as long as China has challenged the hegemony of the United States.

So when Russia, another military power, confronts the United States through the Ukraine war and consumes US' na-

---

[23] Min Suk Kong, Structure of the U.S.-China Conflict: The hegemony competition after the financial crisis, threechairs, 2019, p.89-96.

[24] Historian Niall Ferguson Predicts the Future of China. https://youtu.be/llApVciCScw 2022.2.27.

tional power, the possibility of China being tempted to start a war may increase. Considering the transformation of Xi Jinping into emperor Shi Huangdi, (who should be approved of and pursuing his third term in power in the year 2023, with the possibility of life-long in office following his second term), he may not be able to resist the temptation to start a war as he promised in 2022 to solve the problem of Taiwan.[25] Also, as exclusive information has already been leaked during the Ukraine war, Putin went through communication, notification, and prior coordination with Xi Jinping to start the Ukraine war after the Beijing Winter Olympics. Likewise, it appears that Xi Jinping also communicated with Putin during a meeting that he would invade Taiwan in the fall of this year in 2022, based on the principle of diplomatic reciprocity.[26]

---

[25] Yong Sung Cho, 「The future 10 years of China」, Nexus BIZ, 2012, p.110.

[26] On Feb. 4, 2022, Chinese President Xi Jinping and Russian President Vladimir Putin held a summit in Beijing and issued a joint statement calling for an end to the expansion of NATO. At this summit, China supported opposition to Ukraine's NATO accession, Russia opposed Taiwan's independence and they expressed a unanimous stance on major international issues.

There are mainly two sides to this Ukrainian war. Ukraine's desperate resistance led Russia to a war of attrition, and the United States and Western society did not have to directly intervene except for proxy warfare. Nevertheless, it is already likely that Russia will divide territorially and occupy Ukraine with the capture of Mariupol, a bridgehead linking the Crimea, Luhansk, and Donbas regions. It is not easy to predict whether prudent Xi Jinping will eventually invade Taiwan, further escalating the conflict with the US and turning it into an international war. Nor can we be optimistic about the harsh international order that there will be no war at all. All we can do is pray earnestly for the hope that the invasion of Taiwan and World War III will not happen as the world citizens will be filled with pain and depression.

△ Picture 5　Chinese President Xi Jinping and U.S. President Joe Biden

3 Big Tech[27] vs. Russia, a military power based on geopolitical tradition

There is a view that Russia didn't show itself as the world's second-largest military power(Russia has more nuclear warheads than the US) and even look like forgetting the basic grammar of modern warfare by fighting a clumsy battle at the beginning of this war. In order to lead the war to advantage in modern warfare, it is important to seize or paralyze telecommunications and broadcasting in the war zone. But, news of the war situation, civil society, government governance, and international response are being shared in real-time in Ukraine, up to the current situation in which the war seems to be moving beyond the war of attrition into a long-term war. During the war, legacy media, broadcasting, and communication were not naturally seized or paralyzed. But rather, cameras on personal

---

27 Large technology(IT) companies that owns and operates a digital platform. see [Reference books and information] at the back.

smartphones are sending out to the world the war situation in Ukraine everywhere by one person broadcasting. Even during a national emergency of a war, real-time sites and information are spreading all over the world that is much larger than the information gathering area of public broadcasting.

Is Russia leading the war to defeat like an amateur while starting a war, overlooking the principle of modern warfare that it can be led to advantage only by controlling or destroying the other country's telecommunications and broadcasting? Rather than overlooking the grammar of modern warfare, it is safe to say that even the world's second-largest military and geopolitical power is being hit by big tech. In other ways, they are being attacked by the ability to outperform the geopolitical state power. It is clear that of course, Russia had attempted to take over or blow up Ukraine's telecommunications and broadcasting system in the first place.

Nevertheless, Ukraine's rather young deputy prime minister in his 30s openly tweeted very politely to Elon Musk(the founder of Tesla) to ask launch Starlink, a low-altitude satellite communication system, over Ukraine. Then Elon Musk also left a simple and clear positive response on Twitter. So not only the key communication and broadcasting facilities in the country, but also the internet, telecommunications, and smartphone-based personal broadcasting in the Ukraine territory through the satellite system in space are still available during the war.

Due to the global corona pandemic, the value of the currency has decreased due to a large-scale economic stimulus. Meanwhile, Elon Musk and other so-called big tech groups operated a coin market with Dogecoin, Bitcoin, Ethereum, Altcoin, etc., which is equivalent to gold as an alternative value by bypassing the value of a currency. Thus, as an alternative currency that bypassed state power, they fully revitalized the coin market and led the ups and downs almost like gambling. In fact, Elon Musk seemed pathetic when he pointed to Dogecoin, a coin with a dog symbol, and uses social fame and trust in his fandom and his leading IT technology to infuse and subtract bubble-like vitality repeatedly to the so-called 'dog' coin.[28]

---

[28] https://www.bbc.com/ukrainian/news-60583913

Nevertheless, these types of big-tech companies and related elites were able to gain or amass enormous reflective benefits under the pandemic by making transnational technology platforms more skillful, even under a situation where the totality of state power was insufficient to respond to the pandemic.

In other words, there were many difficult points in solving the virus crisis even the most advanced national powers put all their might into the global pandemic. Until the ability to respond to COVID-19 against humanity was cultivated for nearly two years, there were not many ways to respond other than lock down the society.

Meanwhile, as non-contact social distancing became common due to the pandemic, big tech based on IT platforms tried to suck human authority like a black hole by shouting Metaverse, etc., and pre-empted mankind's future social platform and agenda.

It is no exaggeration to say that Elon Musk(an elite of big tech companies) was one of the biggest contributors to the invasion of Ukraine by making a great blow to Russia(a huge military power country), after or amid the pandemic. The idea he invented and implemented uniquely to spread the Internet to even remote areas, Starlink(a satellite system that enables fast Internet anywhere in the world by densely floating satellites at low altitudes over the earth), was a unique idea. But it was also a plan to mass-produce side effects and incidental problems.

If satellites are launched at high latitudes outside the Earth's atmosphere, the coverage is wide and the number of satellites can be reduced to cover the entire Earth. But the speed is significantly reduced due to the problem of communicating from a long distance. Elon Musk tried to implement a system that guarantees high Internet speed by launching numerous satellites at low altitudes above the Earth, as aggressively and uniquely as Don Quixote style.

The lifespan of the satellites will expire and a lot of space garbage will be mass-produced over time. But it was only an incidental factor outside consideration in the priority of implementing the idea. Also, he was not concerned about the fact that the probability of unexpected accidents increases because of collisions between satellites, and the situation in which astronomical observation for natural science research is obstructed by too many floating satellites. The universe was not an area that can be occupied or influenced by state power like a geopolitical territory anyway. Elon Musk has built a kind of unrestricted technology in a universe outside of state power.

Invented by Elon Musk, called Starlink(Internet communication based on satellites outside the Earth's geopolitical airspace or territory, and the atmosphere) stayed over Ukraine and continued Internet communication. Therefore, Ukraine was able to maximize its counter-resistance capabilities by mobilizing internal affairs through favorable communication for themselves. And they could constantly inform the war situation and seek support and will to resist the war to the international community against the invasion of Russia, even in a war comparable to the fight between Goliath and David. In that sense, to Ukraine, it would not be an exaggeration to say that

Starlink was David's slingshot who defeated Goliath.[29]

Through Starlink, Ukraine was able to broadcast the real-time invasion situation live on TikTok, YouTube, Facebook, and Instagram to the world by going to war without paralyzing or disconnecting real-time internet and telecommunications. The government and the president, and other key figures were also able to inform the injustice of the invasion in real-time at international conferences and meetings with a single smartphone, requesting support and receiving assistance from the international community, and were provided with the real-time situation of Russia's aggression from the US. In addition, citizens are engaged in nonviolent resistance movements in various regions such as Kherson occupied by Russia. They open their smartphone cameras based on alive internet communication as a tool to prove the real-time situation of war crime by the Russian military, and boldly engage in nonviolent civil protests with TikTok, YouTube, Facebook Live, Instagram, etc. in front

---

[29] Global Cooperation Headquarters, 「Digitally Looked Ukraine Russia Situation」, National Information Society Agency, 2022, p.11.

of heavy weapons such as the armed Russian army and tanks who have taken over the city.

While passing through the pandemic and wars at the same time, I anticipate and forecast an era in which big tech companies will bypass, equal to, or exceed traditional state power in the future.[30] The Chinese government, which feels a similar phenomenon as a threat, tends to leave these big tech companies without sanctions or restrictions until they improve some of their technologies for the national interest. However, if there is a possibility of the situation that they can grow uniquely enough to exceed the state power, then check with a kind of soft landing as a pretext, or make reversion to the state power, or even lead to semi-dissolution. Even for the Chinese national government, which controls 1.4 billion people (one-fifth of the world's population), big tech companies have emerged as a target of check because they seem to outperform the state

---

30 After Elon Musk's Starlink support, social media platform companies have taken sanction against Russia, including blocking or labeling Russian state media to prevent the spread of fake news about Ukraine.

power sometimes. Elon Musk applied a duel to Putin in Russia through social media in front of the public, and the comment that they had already been fought can be dismissed as a joke. But it cannot be denied that the battle proceeded without subduing Starlink's role and couldn't take the lead in communication was a major factor in the defeat of the Russian army. I carefully confirmed and foreseen from the side through Russia's invasion of Ukraine and its defeat, that the era is showing signs of huge shift conversion since the pandemic and war.

△ Picture 6 **The CEO of Tesla, Elon Musk's tweet**

4 The blood of war, the price of innocent blood, the possibility of negotiations, truce, and peace

We silently but desperately weigh and measure the weight of the innocent blood sprinkled on Ukraine. Who would be responsible for the price of the blood from innocent Ukrainian citizens (killed in Mariupol and other places) to young Russian soldiers who thought they were training for the first time in the field?

Ukraine, which had an absolute inferior military strength compared to the military power of Russia, got the help of reading the war situation by receiving intelligence in advance from the United States, which read Russia's intention of invasion relatively accurately. Rather than forming a front line on the field, Ukraine prepared for urban fights in Kyiv and other places.

The field battles with many open areas were relatively disadvantageous for Ukrainian forces as they faced Russia, which has a major force in its armored forces. Urban warfare strategy against world powers can be a reasonable option for Ukraine in terms of combat strategy doctrine. Most likely, the US also fully understood that Ukraine's advantageous strategy was to engage in guerrilla warfare from the rear, (the US also suffered a lot in urban warfare, such as the Iraq War and the Battle of Mosul, even with its one-sided military power of absolute superiority). such as cutting off logistics while defending the enemy in the cities including Kyiv, the capital city. Therefore, the West, such as the United States, Britain, and Germany, provided Ukraine with weapons and supplies for urban and armored warfare, and urban warfare soon became one of the main defense strategies of the Ukrainian government. However, the dark side of this inevitable national strategy is that it involves mixing the battlefield with innocent civil society.[31]

---

[31] Major Western countries including the US, have provided more than $3 bilion in military supplies to Ukraine since 2014, and U.S. special operation forces trained Ukrainian army near Lviv in western Ukraine.
https://www.nytimes.com/2022/03/03/us/politics/russia-ukraine-military.html

Comparatively, Russia has experience in possessing or subduing an army relatively familiar with huge urban warfare through the war in Syria and Chechnya.[32] Russia is well aware of the price paid in urban fighting, no matter how superior its army is to its opponents. Rather than allowing the military to enter the city first, Russia use a strategy of indiscriminately firing the city with artilleries or carpet bombing, isolating and destroying the entire city for conquest and drawing out submission.[33] Like the army that surrounded the castle in the Middle Ages, where a castle can also be a town, Russia employs a strategy of completely killing both soldiers and citizens without worrying about the damage.

Kyiv (a metropolis with a population of 4 million) and not to mention Mariupol, is several times larger than the Chechen capital, Grozny, where Putin previously had a history of split-

---

[32] Steven Lee Myers, same as the previous book(2016), p.205-234.
[33] Steven Lee Myers, same as the previous book(2016), p.219, 228.

ting Chechenian nationalists and Islamic fundamentalists,[34] making them submit at the cost of much bloodshed in urban fighting. Also, Modern cities are packed with buildings made of dense concrete that are several times stronger than those of old medieval fortresses. If all the buildings were to be destroyed by bombardment to reveal the enemy forces hiding in each building, it would almost be impossible even with all the Russian artilleries and missiles that exist.

Therefore, this aspect of urban warfare is as brutal as siege warfare of indiscriminate barbarism in the Middle Ages, in that innocent citizens and troops can be mixed in the city front and war situation and be killed together.[35] In addition, considering

---

[34] Walter Laqueur, same as the previous book(2015), p.290-292. Young Hoon Son, 「The development process of the Chechen-Russian War and national terrorism」, 『Conflicts in Post-Soviet Eurasia』, Misokwon, 2014, p.125-130.

[35] According to British Janes statistics, 11,000 Russian forces and Chechenya government forces were killed in the 1st and 2nd Chechenya Wars. In contrast, it is estimated that at least 80,000 civilians were killed in the 2nd Chechenya War, 200,000 by the Chechenya government, and 250,000-300,000 by Chechenya rebels. Even at the minimum level, the number of civilian deaths was about 8 times higher than in the military. Young Hoon Son, same as the previous book(2014), p.140.

that each building can serve as a medieval fortress, the intensity of weapons and violence used in war throughout the city is tens of thousands of times greater than the operation to capture a town or city in the past barbaric medieval wars. Who says that modern warfare has only progressed, refined, and advanced compared to the past? In a sense, modern warfare is more cold-hearted, brutal, and even barbaric than the sum of seizure, violence, barbarism, and shame all combined during ancient and medieval times.

Russia is also a world-power that can use overwhelming violence. Considering the huge price that Russia will have to pay (even if it wins the urban fight), the cost of using elite ground forces, indiscriminate carpet bombing, and artilleries is higher than our imagination. This may make Russia difficult to resist the temptation to mobilize more barbaric means to subdue the city. Rather than pouring more than trillions of dollars on missiles, Russia is inflicting extermination through lethal but simple chemical warfare and causing irreparable damage to cities through the use of small nuclear warheads. Therefore, the fact that urban warfare (whether it's offense or defense) is considered or adopted as a strategic element in modern times (with the tendency towards enlargement of cities or metropolia) is already accompanied by great blood and evil.

Mariupol has already become a ghost town and a victim of urban fighting due to numerous bombardments and firing. Many of Kyiv's residents have become refugees. They are trembling in fear as they are being bombed in the suburbs of the capital and even apartments and shopping malls in downtown areas.

While witnessing this brutality in real-time, what the global civil society desperately hopes for is a ceasefire and peace through negotiations between the two countries. However, the reality of international society is not so romantic. The element that establishes an agreement and an armistice in a war situation are not that the national ethic for peace is at work. It is rather similar to gangster society, where gangs negotiate or reach an agreement when the violence has reached the threshold. Negotiation starts when a territorial dispute has already begun, the stabbing occurred and much blood is shed enough to cause a burden on the gang or the group.

Russia has not even started bringing in and using its Syrian troops accustomed to the Syrian civil war. Russia drew out the division between Chechen nationalists and Islamic fundamentalists in the Chechen War, destroying the anti-Russian Chechen army, and using the remaining pro-Russian Chechen forces as mercenaries as one of the main forces in Mariupol. Putin has a history and pride in persistently carrying his point and subduing Chechen (a nation developed from a small tribe), through a ten-year long-term war.[36] Ukraine can be conquered only by

---

[36] In fact, Putin's approval rating also rose during the same period. At the time Putin was appointed Prime Minister (September 1999), the support for the next presidential candidate was around 2% in opinion polls, but after the outbreak of the Second Chechen War (September 1999), it rose to 27% in October.
Steven Lee Myers, same as the previous book(2016), p.221-223.

subjugating numerous cities of Ukraine, which is several times larger than Chechnya, and this causes attrition for Russia. But even if Russia fails, it will not back down at all to carry out the idea of conquering and linking Crimea, Donbas, and Luhansk. If Russia wants to subdue the whole of Ukraine, including Kyiv, it's a matter of attrition. Therefore, Russia already has the most brutal but handy cards (it's just that the cause is unjust and vicious towards humanity) in the history of mankind, such as chemical warfare and small nuclear warheads, As long as the war has already begun, whatever their decision may be will risk a huge amount of blood and price.

What can replace the blood of those who died innocently? Those who have lost their families do not only grieve over their city, but their world turning upside down.

Meanwhile, nonviolent protests by Ukrainian citizens whose cities have been invaded are a bold and courageous choice because the citizens face an army that can use violence by any means during wartime, and they stand up unarmed against heavy weapons. However, it is sad and heartbreaking that they even risk shedding the blood of themselves and their families. The same goes for those left behind and millions of people who suddenly became refugees during the war and were driven away as if wandering to a foreign country, losing their families and homes, and having to leave their hometowns and countries where they do not know when they would return.

Now that modern warfare (which is becoming increasingly brutal), is shared or witnessed in real-time with the development of social media, should we become cold-hearted spectators who leave comments online? Witnessing the blood of innocent lives that will be flooding as we get closer to long-term warfare, and the edgy lives of countless refugees who have lost their families and homes, what are we, Christians, people of peace doing? Does this blood of war have nothing to do with us Christians because the violence is not our fault? Through prayer, we can hold the key to heaven and connect the world with Christ, the Sovereign of Heaven, in peace. We can also act/move and serve according to His will, so that refugees who have lost their home, hometown, and country can converge to God's love, hometown, and country. Through the gospel, we can purify the blood of the kings and nations of the world with the blood of Christ. Now is the time to pray and act together for peace. We hope that the joint action of Christ's ambassadors for peace goes deeper and wider than that cruel frontline of war.

5 Conclusion
Our responsibilities
– Between crisis and disaster, Is Christianity without prospects? Is Christianity with a vision?

We see that the Christian heritage is moving rapidly towards the relief of Ukraine refugees and the war. It is often to hear that Christian missionaries are taking care of the locals even during the war and opening a route for help and cooperation with the international community by going to neighboring countries. It is also true that the Christians who embrace the love of Christ, are quick to act together in the midst of a world crisis. However, if there is one disappointment, although signs of conflict have already been at odds with Ukraine government due to the Crimean Peninsula incident and the establishment of pro-Russian autonomous governments in Donetsk and Luhansk[37] 10 years ago, I've hardly ever heard of signs of war or co-existence of crisis from any Christian channel.

Isn't Christianity a religion of vision for the future beyond academic prospects? Abraham saw and heard in advance from God in a vision that the people of Israel(who were slaves in Egypt) cried out for rescue during their crisis and eventually return to the land of Canaan after 400 years even though Pharaoh refused and hindered liberation because of his toughness.[38] God revealed His power is over Pharaoh's toughness by striking all the firstborns in the land of Egypt. God foresaw that Cyrus would encourage the migration of the ruled peoples to their homeland and settlement according to their indigenous culture due to increased tax revenues in the territory for his power. He made Jeremiah proclaim the vision in advance that Israel

---

[37] In April 2014, pro-Russian forces in Luhansk and Donetsk declared their independence respectively into the Lugansk People's Republic (LPR, Луганская Народная Республика) and the Donetsk People's Republic (DPR, Донецкая Народная). All of them are currently unrecognized states.

[38] Genesis 15:13-14

will return to their homeland 70 years after the Babylonian exilic period.[39]

Missions emphasized regional studies and R&D to understand and research the field first in order to save the mission field. Indeed, the field where wars and disasters occur beyond the crisis, would be destroyed and damaged with an enormous loss of life. How come the missionary society couldn't give little warning of war in Ukraine, the gateway and hub for Christian propagation in Eastern Europe while they are emphasizing field-oriented research? In some senses, missionary resources who can understand and study the field and operate them as the kingdom of God, have been sent to the field of Eastern Europe, Ukraine, and Russia as much as oversea student resources for studying Eastern Europe. Then why did we hardly predict the crisis in Ukraine at all? Academics also play a role in prospects, and from the Crimean conflict to the Donbas war, and even wars over China and Taiwan have already been studied, reported, or warned until 2021. But in the Christianity world, the

---

[39] Jeremiah 29:10

crisis was only recognized and dealt with through the media when it surfaced during invasion of Ukraine in 2022, like 'After death comes a doctor.' There are hardly any reports of an urgent global situation through the Christian R&D Institute, or Institute of International Studies/Regional Studies for Missions.

In addition, if China's invasion of Taiwan occurs in a series of wars in Eastern Europe after the pandemic crisis, the damage to the mission movement beyond the continent will be very serious with the erosion of the Christian heritage.

In history, World Wars 1 and 2 broke out during the heyday of the Western mission movement. We must not forget the historical lesson that young missionary volunteers from all over Europe gathered and trained to participate in the mission movement due to saving lives, were conscripted, and drifted into a war where they fought and killed each other with their guns.

As Xi Jinping has declared, even if China invades Taiwan, it will act as a decisive blow to the mission movement in Asia including the Korean Peninsula, while Christianity in non-Western countries in Asia grows, expands, and matures.

Xi Jinping first heard Putin's plan to invade Ukraine during the Beijing Winter Olympics and mutually informed Putin about the invasion of Taiwan in the fall. I warn you again, If China's invasion of Taiwan became a known fact, Xi Jinping will say the dispute between Taiwan and China is nothing more than internal conflict and civil war within the same ethnic group, to create justifications to burden the international community's intervention, even he has in mind that the US and Japan would intervene in the war to secure the Taiwan Strait.[40] Including the West countries that have already established diplomatic ties with China, premise that they do not recognize Taiwan as a state. Therefore, it should be noted that Xi Jinping can create a justification for war internally and externally even though he knows the backlash of the international community if the interests are aligned like Putin. Nevertheless, it is the Lord who rules

---

40 Min Suk Kong, Structure of the U.S.—China Conflict: The hegemony competition after the financial crisis, threechairs, 2019. p.81.

the hearts of Putin and Xi Jinping and works in people's hearts, nations, and the world on options such as their interests and desires, like what He did to Pharaoh and Cyrus. He also informs people of faith about the vision and warnings of the times and leads them to turn catastrophes between crises and disasters.

Even if China chooses war in succession following Russia, it is the Lord who will turn evil into good again through the prayers of people of faith, cooperation for peace, relief for those embroiled in war, and international coordination. However, it is obvious that the catastrophe and destruction would be very serious if we just face the situation in which huge death is more prevalent than life due to a series of wars between the West, East Asia, and Eurasia after the pandemic. We must first gather the prayers of Christians to prevent war and catastrophe By forecasting and warning.

If even China chooses war following Russia, it goes without saying that we will face a disaster that feels like a curse through another direct and indirect world war centered in East Asia, such as Taiwan, the US, Japan, Russia, North Korea, and South Korea. Then, it seems obvious that the plan such as the declaration of a neutral country in order not to be swept away by the gang war, will be a naive and ingenuous countermeasure when we face the reality of the logic of the ruthless force and dynamics in the international community. The international order will forcefully demand that join the war on each side of the Korean Peninsula, not only the Republic of Korea but also North Korea. China has long ago envisioned and implemented the challenge of escaping from the hegemony of the US, and the US has already prepared swiftly to confront China and has compressed and tightened most of its national power like a spring for a long time to overwhelm the confrontation.(Even if it is not the case in 2021, China and the US are highly likely to collide structurally in our time.)[41] If the war begins, it is clear that Christianity in non-Western East Asia, including the Korean Peninsula, will be significantly eroded or drifted away due to the war and its aftereffects during the stagnation or retreat of the Christian her-

---

[41] Min Suk Kong, same as the previous book(2019). p.108.

itage in the West.[42]

Therefore, it is dangerous and irresponsible to have a sense of history that ignores the warning while anticipating and recognizing the precursors of such a crisis, and times will pass without a prospect even for believers. It is necessary to warn them before the times and pray for them to turn around for the Lord to prevent evil before a crisis becomes a disaster and catastrophe. Regarding the evil that has occurred, need to serve refugees and afflicted countries with relief, etc. through united joint action.

Also, not only this time, rumors of war and wars will always be between the nations, then Christians must have a responsibility to expand the vision of the kingdom of God that is bigger than the kingdoms of the world, and the vision of peace and hope of the gospel that transcends the world and times, until the end.

---

[42] In January 2008, a report by the Rand Institute(a non-profit research institute in the US), included South Korea's Osan and Gunsan among the targets of a preemptive surprise attack by the Chinese military to block the US approach in the event of an armed conflict between the US and China over the Taiwan issue.
Yong Sung Cho, same as the previous book(2012), p.112.

6 The direction of prayer to be with you

1) May the Lord will stop the threat of war and war escalation that Russia and China can choose in any possibility, and the prayers of the believers rise like wildfires for the Lord who presides over the thoughts of Pharaoh and Cyrus king of Persia to bring disaster and catastrophe back to the minds of Putin, Xi Jinping, and other rulers.

2) May the Lord will make missionaries and Christians rise in Ukraine and other parts of Eastern Europe with Korean churches to serve Ukrainian refugees and those in the middle of the war, and show that the kingdom of God is the heavenly home of love, peace, and comfort.

3) May the Lord's lamp does not go to shine the light of Jesus toward darkness, and raise and send workers to harvest the

world with glory, while the world has gone through crises such as infectious diseases and wars, even during Christian missionary inheritance weakened and destroyed.

4) May the kingdom of God of justice, love, and peace, which work and make history beyond the world and the international order, be proclaimed and reigned among all nations and people, so that the kingdom of God is completed, and eternal Shalom and peace may be achieved throughout the world.

Reference books and information

Bains, P., Sugimoto, N., Wilson, C., 2022, 「BigTech in financial services: Regulatory approaches and architecture」, Fintech note 2022/002, IMF.

Benedict R. O'G. Anderson, 「Imagined Communities: Reflections on the Origin and Spread of Nationalism」, 1983.

Boissay, F., Ehlers, T., Gambacorta, L., Shin, H.S., 2021, 「Big techs in finance: on the new nexus between data privacy and competition」, BIS working papes No.970.

Byung-Ock Chang, 「Articles : International Society ; The Conflict History of Chechnya-Russia - Focusing on Chechen's Islamist」, 「International Area Studies Review」, 13(1), The International Association of Area Studies, 2009, 513-530.

Carstens, A., Claessens, S., Restoy, F., Shin, H.S., 2021, 「Regulating big techs in finance」, BIS Bulletin No.45.

Crisanto, J.C., Ehrentraud, J., Lawson, A., Restoy, F., 2021, 「Big tech regulations: what is going on?」, FSI insights on policy implementation No.36, BIS.

E. J. Hobsbawm, 「Nations and Nationalism since 1780」, Cambridge University Press, 2012.

E J Hobsbawm, Terence O. Ranger, 「The Invention of Tradition」, Cambridge University Press, 1983.

Gao Xiao, Continental Leader Xi Jinping, translated by Ha Jin Yi, Samho Media, 2012

Gat Azar, Yacobson Alexander, 「Nations: The Long History and Deep Roots of Political Ethnicity and Nationalism」, Cambridge University Press, 2012.

Geun-wook Lee, 「War in Afghanistan」, Hanul Academy, 2021.

George Friedman, 「Flashpoints: The Emerging Crisis in Europe」, Anchor Books, 2016.

Gérard Chaliand, Sophie Mousset, 「Question kurde :à l'heure de Daech」, Hanul, 2018.

Global Cooperation Headquarters, 「Digitally Looked Ukraine Russia Situation」, National Information Society Agency, 2022.

Hanyang University Asia Pacific Research Center Russia and Eurasia Research Group, 「Conflicts in Post-Soviet Eurasia」, Minsokwon, 2014.

Hanyang University Asia Pacific Research Center Russia Eurasia Research Group, 「Eurasia's national and ethnic identity」, Hanul Academy, 2010.

Hans-Peter Martin, 「Game Over - Wohlstand fur wenige, Demokratie fur niemand, Nationalismus fur alle - und dann?」, Penguin Verlag Munchen, 2018.

Hyun Seung-soo, Terrorism and conflict escalation in the Russian Federation's North Kavkaz, Conflicts in Post-Soviet Eurasia, Minsokwon, 2014

KBS Documentary Insight Pandemic Money Production Team, 「Pandemic money」, Readers book, 2021.

Margareta Mommsen, 「Das Putin-Syndikat (Russland im Griff der Geheimdienstler)」, C.H.Beck, 2017.

Min Suk Kong, Structure of the U.S.-China Conflict: The hegemony competition after the financial crisis, threechairs, 2019.

Niall Ferguson, 「Doom: The Politics of Catastrophe」, Penguin Press, 2021.

Pascal Boniface, 「Geopolitics What is happening in the world right now?」, Guardian, 2019.

Sang Ho, Son, 「Eight Challenges for Financial Innovation」, Korea Institute of Finance, 2022.

Sejin Jung, 「Regional Studies: A Study on the Formation of the Identity of the Chechen People」, 「Journal of Russian Literature Research」, 44 Vol., Korean Association of Rusists, p.507-537, 2013.

Sejin Jung, 「Russia Islam(History, ideology, war)」, Minsokwon, 2014.

Sejin Jung, 「Происхождение Чеченской войны-через исторические конфликты между Россиии и Чечни」, 「The Journal of Slavic Studies」, Vol.20 No.2, The Korean association of Slavic-Eurasian Studies, 2005, 355-386.

Seong-jin Kim, 「Frozen Conflict in Moldova: Its Developments and Background」, 「Conflicts in Post-Soviet Eurasia」, Minsokwon, 2014.

Shin, H.S., 2019, 「Big tech in finance: opportunities and risks」, BIS Annual Economic Report.

Steven Lee Myers, 「The New Tsar: The Rise and Reign of Vladimir Putin」, Vintage Books USA, 2016.

Sung Hoon Cho, 「Competition Policy for Big Techs and their Entry into Financial Services」, 「Capital Market Focus」, 2022-06, Korea Capital Market Institute.

Wan Suk Hong, 「A Rough Road Ahead, Conflicts Between Russia and Chechenya : Causes, Developments and Prospect」, 「The Korean Political Science Association」, 39(5), 2005, 237-262.

Walter Laqueur, 「Putinism: Russia and Its Future with the West」, Thomas Dunne Books, 2015.

Yang Hyun Tak, 「Russian History: Principality of Kiev Rus Moscow, Russian Empire, Soviet Union, Russian Federation」, ePubple, 2020.

Young Hoon Son, 「The development process of the Chechen-Russian War and national terrorism」, 「Conflicts in Post-Soviet Eurasia」, Misokwon, 2014, 117.

Yong Sung Cho, 「The future 10 years of China」, Nexus BIZ, 2012.

Limbach, Raymond. "Battle of Stalingrad". Encyclopedia Britannica, 15 Aug. 2021, https://www.britannica.com/event/Battle-of-Stalingrad. Accessed 6 April 2022.

Historian Niall Ferguson Predicts the Future of China. https://youtu.be/IIApVciCScw 2022.2.27.

Yuval Noah Harari, 「Why Vladimir Putin has already lost this war」, 「The Guardian Weekly」, 2022.03.28., https://www.theguardian.com/commentisfree/2022/feb/28/vladimir-putin-war-russia-ukraine

https://www.bbc.com/ukrainian/news-60583913

https://www.nytimes.com/2022/03/03/us/politics/russia-ukraine-military.html